Plagiarism

Heidi Williams, *Book Editor*

GREENHAVEN PRESS
A part of Gale, Cengage Learning

GALE
CENGAGE Learning™

Detroit • New York • San Francisco • New Haven, Conn • Waterville, Maine • London

Christine Nasso, *Publisher*
Elizabeth Des Chenes, *Managing Editor*

© 2008 Greenhaven Press, a part of Gale, Cengage Learning

For more information, contact:
Greenhaven Press
27500 Drake Rd.
Farmington Hills, MI 48331-3535
Or you can visit our Internet site at http://gale.cengage.com

For product information and technology assistance, contact us at

Gale Customer Support, 1-800-877-4253
For permission to use material from this text or product, submit all requests online at
www.cengage.com/permissions

Further permissions questions can be emailed to permissionrequest@cengage.com

Articles in Greenhaven Press anthologies are often edited for length to meet page requirements. In addition, original titles of these works are changed to clearly present the main thesis and to explicitly indicate the author's opinion. Every effort is made to ensure that Greenhaven Press accurately reflects the original intent of the authors. Every effort has been made to trace the owners of copyrighted material.

Cover image © Damir Karan, 2008. Used under license from Shutterstock.com

LIBRARY OF CONGRESS CATALOGING-IN-PUBLICATION DATA

Plagiarism / Heidi Williams, book editor.
   p. cm. — (Issues that concern you)
  Includes bibliographical references and index.
   ISBN-13: 978-0-7377-4072-1 (hardcover)
 1. Plagiarism. I. Williams, Heidi.
  PN167.P523 2008
  808—dc22

                                        2008004531

Printed in the United States of America
2 3 4 5 6 7 12 11 10 09 08

CONTENTS

INTRODUCTION

Writing is difficult, and being a good writer involves count-less skills. Besides spelling and grammar, which seem like enough to worry about, good writing involves finding your writing voice, expressing your own ideas, and in many cases incorporating other people's ideas into the mix. When you need to support your opinion with the ideas and expertise of others, writing gets even more difficult, becomes more time-consuming, and plagiarism becomes very tempting.

Plagiarism is not just a middle or high school issue. In recent years, famous journalists, top-ten novelists, university professors and administrators, and even pastors have succumbed to it.

The *New York Times*, one of the most respected newspapers in the United States, rocked the journalism world when its noted feature writer, Jayson Blair, was found to have made up facts and quotes or plagiarized in over thirty articles over a seven-month period, some of them front-page stories. He blamed his unethical behavior on his past use of drugs and bipolar disorder.

Steven King, J.K. Rowling, and Dan Brown, three of the most celebrated popular fiction writers of our time, have all been taken to civil court, accused of stealing ideas from other writers. They all claimed innocence.

Kaavya Viswanathan, while a freshman at Harvard University, wrote a novel that was climbing its way up the *New York Times* Best Sellers list for hardcover fiction when it was discovered that she had taken long passages directly from another novel. After her publisher pulled her books and canceled future contracts, additional plagiarized passages from other novels were found. Viswanathan claimed that the obvious copying was accidental, a result of her very good memory.

Janet Dailey is the best-selling author of almost one hundred romance novels, which have been translated into nineteen languages and have reached sales numbers of more than 2 million

Plagiarism is the intentional copying of another's words or ideas without attribution, and it happens both inside and outside the classroom.

copies. When accused of copying from the work of Nora Roberts, another prolific romance writer, she confessed but claimed that her acts of plagiarism were due to a mental illness.

A chancellor at Southern Illinois University was forced to leave his position over accusations that he had imported sections of a long-range plan that he had written for SIU from a similar document that he had written while at another school. Previously at SIU, a professor was fired for plagiarizing his philosophy of teaching statement. As of this writing, SIU president Glenn Poshard, a former congressman and candidate for governor of Illinois, is under fire for alleged plagiarism in his doctoral dissertation. Multiple passages were taken directly from other writers without paraphrasing, quotation marks, or citations.

Poshard does not deny the allegations but excuses himself, claiming ignorance of the rules of citation and an overwhelmingly busy life at the time.

In recent years many prominent pastors have been found guilty of plagiarizing sermons: Robert Hamm, senior pastor of Keene United Church of Christ in Keene, New Hampshire; Glenn Wagner, pastor of Calvary Church in Charlotte, North Carolina; Alvin O'Neal Jackson, pastor of Park Avenue Christian Church in Manhattan; Edward Mullins, rector of Christ Church Cranbrook in West Bloomfield, Michigan; and Lawrence Biondi, Jesuit priest and president of St. Louis University are just a few. Excuses given are lack of time, emotional duress, and the pressure from their congregations to be as engaging as the writers from whom they are plagiarizing.

Is plagiarism becoming more common, more detectable, or more acceptable? The outcomes of some of the cases listed above may be surprising.

The *New York Times* writer Jayson Blair was fired along with some of his bosses. Blair, however, has since written a book about his experience and now guest lectures about ethics in journalism.

The cases against Steven King, J.K. Rowling, and Dan Brown were thrown out for lack of evidence, and Rowling's accuser was found to have fabricated evidence and fined thirty thousand dollars.

Kaavya Viswanathan's novel was recalled, and she lost her contract for a sequel but remained at Harvard.

Upon her admission of guilt, Janet Dailey settled out of court with Nora Roberts for an undisclosed amount of money, which Roberts donated to a pro-literacy organization. Less than five years later, however, Dailey had contracts to write eight more books and sold the rights to fifty of her previously published romance novels.

At Southern Illinois University, as mentioned, the professor who lifted his philosophy of teaching statement was fired, and the chancellor who copied his own strategic plan resigned under pressure; however, the current university president and former congressman, who plagiarized portions of his dissertation, remains in his position.

Plagiarizing pastors have seen mixed fates. Some have resigned, some have been fired, and some have been given a second chance.

The matter of plagiarism seems like it should be black and white, and sometimes it is, but not always. Where does inspiration end and plagiarism begin? Who is ultimately responsible when plagiarism shows up—the student or the teacher? What is the best strategy for stopping it? Can it even be avoided?

Plagiarism is definitely in the news and a matter worthy of discussion for professionals as well as today's students. The articles in this volume represent multiple viewpoints surrounding the issue. It is hoped that they will help you understand the issue more fully, yet also see it in its full complexity.

ONE

Plagiarism Once Was Considered Acceptable

Brian Hansen

Each issue of the *CQ Researcher* provides unbiased in-depth information on one important controversial topic. The author, Brian Hansen, was once a staff writer for *CQ Researcher* specializing in social-policy issues and, prior to that, was a newspaper reporter and a reporter for the Environment News Service in Washington. In the following viewpoint Hansen explains the history and development of people's attitudes toward ownership of the written word. From ancient Greece to the invention of the printing press to the United States' first universities to the current day, he traces the evolution of the concept of plagiarism.

Plagiarism has not always been regarded as unethical. In fact, for most of recorded history, drawing from other writers' works was encouraged. This view was grounded in the belief that knowledge of the human condition should be shared by everyone, not owned or hoarded. The notion of individual authorship was much less important than it is today.

"Writers strove, even consciously, to imitate earlier great works," wrote authors Peter Morgan and Glenn Reynolds in their 1997 book *The Appearance of Impropriety*. "That a work

Brian Hansen, "Combating Plagiarism," *CQ Researcher*, September 19, 2003, pp. 782–787. Copyright © 2003 by CQ Press, published by CQ Press, a division of Congressional Quarterly Inc. All rights reserved. Reproduced by permission.

had obvious parallels with an early work—even similar passages or phrases—was a mark of pride, not plagiarism. Imitation was bad only when it was disguised or a symptom of laziness. It was not denounced simply on the grounds of being 'unoriginal.'"

Examples of this tradition abound in literature. In ancient Greece, for example, writers such as Homer, Plato, Socrates and Aristotle borrowed heavily from earlier works. "Aristotle lifted whole pages from Democritus," wrote Alexander Lindey in his 1952 book *Plagiarism and Originality*.

Novelist and former Vassar College English Professor Thomas Mallon agrees that the concept of originality was radically different centuries ago. "Jokes about out-and-out literary theft go back all the way to Aristophanes and 'The Frogs' [a play written in 405 B.C.], but what we call plagiarism was more a matter for laughter than litigation," Mallon wrote in his 1989 book *Stolen Words: Forays into the Origins and Ravages of Plagiarism*. "The Romans rewrote the Greeks. Virgil is, in a broadly imitative way, Homer, and for that matter, typologists can find most of the Old Testament in the New."

The Greek concept of imitation—known as *mimesis*—continued to influence writers during the Middle Ages. According to Syracuse [University's Rebecca] Moore Howard, the Catholic Church promoted the medieval emphasis on mimesis because it was concerned with spreading the message of God. "The individual writer in this economy of authorship is beside the point, even a hindrance," Howard writes in her 1999 book *Standing in the Shadow of Giants: Plagiarists, Authors, Collaborators*. "Instead, the writer voices God's truth . . . and participates in the tradition of that truth-telling. Even in patron-sponsored writing for the purpose of entertainment, the writer's identity and originality are only tangentially at issue. Plagiarism was a concern that seldom arose."

Rise of Copyright

Attitudes about plagiarism began to change in the 16th century, as the Protestant Reformation swept across Western Europe. The notion that salvation could be attained without adhering to strict

Catholic sacraments gave new importance to the concepts of originality and individual thought. These ideals were spread far and wide through the use of the printing press—invented in 1440—and new copyright laws, which advanced the notion that individual authorship was good and that mimesis was bad.

Notably, religious reformers like Martin Luther were among the staunchest opponents of the new copyright laws—first proposed in the late 1400s—because they believed human learning should circulate unrestricted for the common good and betterment of mankind.

"Much like defenders of Internet freedoms of access and speech today, Luther and others objected that copyright laws would limit the free circulation of ideas and knowledge that had been made so widely and instantly available . . . [by] the printing press," scholar C. Jan Swearingen wrote in a 1999 essay.

Passage of the first copyright laws—in England in 1710 and in the United States in 1790—transformed writing into a viable economic pursuit. Mimesis was no longer tolerated or encouraged—in fact it was illegal. "No longer was a writer supposed to build on top of the structures left by earlier figures; now one was supposed to sweep the ground clear and build from scratch," Morgan and Reynolds write. "Once money was involved, people became more vigilant for copying, whether real or imagined."

Mallon agrees. "Plagiarism didn't become a truly sore point with writers until they thought of writing as their trade," he writes in *Stolen Words*. "The writer, a new professional, was invented by a machine [the printing press]. Suddenly his capital and identity were at stake. Things were now competitive and personal, and when writers thought they'd been plundered they fought back."

"Fertile Ground"

Meanwhile, other forces were creating "fertile ground for plagiarism" at America's colleges and universities, explains Sue Carter, an associate professor of English at Ohio's Bowling Green State University. Admissions started rising dramatically in the mid-1800s, in part because schools began accepting women for the first time. As enrollments increased, schools began requiring students to present more of their work in writing, rather than orally, as they had in the past, Carter says.

"At Harvard . . . by the 1890s, first-year students wrote a new paper every two weeks as well as one short paper six days a week for the entire academic year," Carter wrote in a 1999 article on the history of plagiarism. "In such a climate . . . students may have felt plagiarism to be a viable option."

Aside from the sheer volume of writing, students also may have felt pushed toward plagiarism because many schools assigned unimaginative, "canned topics" for those papers, Carter says.

Southern Illinois University president Glenn Poshard and his wife, Jo, attend a committee meeting regarding the accusation that Poshard plagiarized parts of his 1984 doctoral dissertation.

"Some students believed it was OK to cheat because the teachers weren't doing their jobs. For them, it made sense to plagiarize."

To be sure, not all the student plagiarism of the mid-19th century was intentional. There were no universally agreed-upon guidelines for using sources properly. Writer's manuals didn't appear until the late 19th or early 20th centuries. "It's not like there was an *MLA Handbook* or a *Chicago Manual of Style*," Carter says. "Students knew they couldn't claim another person's words as their own, but there was nothing to give them specific, concrete guidelines about avoiding plagiarism, such as using quotation marks or footnotes."

Still, students who were so inclined in the mid-1800s could easily obtain completed papers from fraternity houses or "term-paper mills" that set up shop near many universities. A graduate student who taught writing at Harvard in the 1890s even sold term papers himself, Carter says.

Inadvertent academic plagiarism began to level off in the 1920s, as specialized handbooks began to appear providing guidelines on the correct use of sources. Even so, the number of students who patronized term-paper mills continued to grow. Calling themselves academic "research" companies, they advertised in campus newspapers and "alternative" publications and often employed graduate students to do the writing.

In Boston in the 1960s and '70s, for example, term papers were hawked on street corners and from Volkswagen buses, says Kevin Carleton, assistant vice president for public relations at Boston University (BU). "You could find them in Kenmore Square and Harvard Square and at Boston College and Northeastern University," Carleton says.

In 1972, BU sued several local term-paper mills for fraud and won an injunction prohibiting them from operating. The following year, the Massachusetts legislature banned the sale of term papers. Today, 16 states ban term-paper mills, according to the Denver-based National Conference of State Legislatures.

But BU wasn't so successful in 1997 when it tried to use federal anti-racketeering laws to prohibit all term-paper mills from using the fledgling Internet. A federal court dismissed the university's suit on the grounds that the Internet-based mills could not be prosecuted under the racketeering law. The judge also ruled that the university could not prove that it had been substantially harmed by the mills, since it could name only one student who tried to pass off an Internet-purchased paper as his own.

The mills named in the suit had planned to mount a free-speech defense, but they didn't have to use it. "We prepared a very strong First Amendment stance," said Boston lawyer Harvey Schwartz, who represented two of the operations. "This case was about academic freedom on the Internet."

Second Chances

As in the literary and academic worlds, attitudes toward plagiarism also have changed over time in the realm of journalism. "Twenty or 30 years ago, there was plenty of plagiarism, embellishment and other ethical shortcuts," said Howard Kurtz, media critic for *The Washington Post*. "But they didn't always come to light, in part because journalists were reluctant to expose one another."

The University of Maryland's [Thomas] Kunkel agrees. "When I first broke into the business 30 years ago, I worked with a guy who once in a while made up quotes and things," Kunkel recalls. "It was in high-school sports, and he sort of viewed it as saving everybody's time because the quotes were so predictable and innocuous. I don't think his editors knew, but it was pretty common knowledge in newsrooms around the county that there were people who did stuff like that."

In 1972, for example, the now-defunct *National Observer* fired journalist Nina Totenberg for lifting without attribution several paragraphs from a *Washington Post* profile of Rep. Thomas P. "Tip" O'Neill, D-Mass., who was about to become House majority leader. "I was in a hurry. I used terrible judgment," Totenberg said in a 1995 interview. "I should have been punished. I have a strong feeling that a young reporter is entitled to one mistake and to have the holy bejeezus scared out of her to never do it again."

Totenberg got a second chance and today is a well-regarded legal-affairs correspondent for National Public Radio.

Other high-profile cases in which admitted or alleged plagiarists returned to journalism after their work was questioned include:

- **Mike Barnicle**, the legendary *Boston Globe* columnist, resigned in 1998 amid allegations of plagiarism and fabricating articles. Today he writes a column for the *New York Daily News* and frequently appears on MSNBC's "Hardball" and other television programs.

- **Elizabeth Wurtzel** was fired by *The Dallas Morning News* in 1988 for plagiarism. Wurtzel went on to write for prestigious magazines such as *New York* and *The New Yorker*. She has also written two best-selling books, *Prozac Nation: Young and Depressed in America* (1994) and *Bitch: In Praise of Difficult Women* (1999).

- **Marcia Stepanek** was fired by *Business Week* magazine in January 2001 for plagiarizing a *Washington Post* article on computer privacy. Stepanek said she did not intend to plagiarize. "I was sloppy with my notes but nothing more," she said. Today, she is the executive editor of *CIO Insight*, a magazine for information-technology professionals.

Stephen Glass, who was fired by *The New Republic* in 1998 for plagiarizing and fabricating articles, also has cashed in on his wrongdoing. His "novel" about his exploits, *The Fabulist*, was published in May [2003]. It recounts the misadventures of a young writer named Stephen Glass who gets fired from a Washington, D.C.–based magazine for making up news stories and features. The protagonist—like the real Glass—even creates bogus voice-mail recordings and Web sites to conceal his deceit. . . .

Charles Lane, the editor who fired Glass from *The New Republic* in 1998, said he was stunned "that someone could do what Steve did and cash in on it."

"Being disgraced is not so bad these days," said [Kelly] McBride, at the Poynter Institute. "In our society . . . people can capitalize on values [such as] cleverness, creativity, glibness, sharp-tongued wit and cynicism. It really says something about the entertainment society we live in—in that world, we don't really care how smarmy you are."

TWO

Plagiarism Is Not the Same as Copyright Violation

K. Matthew Dames

K. Matthew Dames is the executive editor of Copycense, an online publication that reports on the law, business, and technology of digital content. He is uniquely qualified to comment on digital-content laws, holding both library and information science and law degrees. Along with speaking to librarians about intellectual property issues, he teaches copyright and licensing at Syracuse University's iSchool. In the following viewpoint he compares and contrasts copyright infringement and plagiarism. He explains that copyright violation is a legal issue that can result in lawsuits, fines, and jail time and that plagiarism, idea theft, is not governed by the law but can be even more damaging to someone's professional reputation. He cautions the reader that the issue of plagiarism is gaining more attention, and consequently students, scholars, and writers are being more closely watched. He advises that the best precaution is to understand and follow the rules for giving credit to sources used.

Ohio University, the oldest public university in the state of Ohio, is an institution with an enrollment of about 20,000 students. For the past year [2006], the university has been besieged by a crippling plagiarism scandal. Based on an alumnus'

K. Matthew Dames, "Understanding Plagiarism and How It Differs from Copyright Infringement," *Computers in Libraries*, June 2007, pp. 25–27. Reproduced by permission.

allegations that more than 30 students in the school's mechanical engineering department have plagiarized substantial or core portions of their graduate theses, the Athens, Ohio, institution has ordered those students to address the allegations or risk having their degrees revoked. Some of these theses are 20 years old, according to an article about the case in *The Wall Street Journal* (*WSJ*) on Aug. 15, 2006.

This front-page story was the latest in a series of plagiarism stories that seem to be destined for headline news. According to a *WSJ* article published on May 14, 2006, the board of directors at defense contractor Raytheon Co. decided it would withhold a salary increase and reduce incentive stock compensation to CEO William Swanson after it was revealed that *Swanson's Unwritten Rules of Management*, a booklet he authored, contained

Parts of Harvard University student Kaavya Viswanathan's novel How Opal Mehta Got Kissed, Got Wild, and Got a Life *were suspected of being plagiarized from Sophie Kinsella's* Can You Keep a Secret?

almost verbatim passages from *The Unwritten Rules of Engineering*, a 1944 book by W.J. King.

A few weeks earlier, publisher Little, Brown and Co. took the extraordinary step of removing the novel *How Opal Mehta Got Kissed, Got Wild, and Got a Life* from retail shelves after *The Harvard Crimson* published a story accusing author Kaavya Viswanathan, a Harvard undergraduate student, of pilfering significant portions of two teen novels written by Megan McCafferty, according to a *WSJ* article published on April 28.

Based on these developments, plagiarism has become the new piracy. Just as piracy was a few years ago, plagiarism has become the hot, new crime du jour—an act that suggests immorality and often scandal at once. What's more, plagiarism allegations feed into our society's *Candid Camera* mentality—our seemingly insatiable need to uncover wrongdoing. So that's why I wanted to compare plagiarism and copyright, and to write about the role of information professionals in raising the collective level of citation savvy.

Copyright Does Not Equal Plagiarism

One of the biggest misconceptions about plagiarism is that it is synonymous with copyright infringement. Each passing year, I spend more time during my copyright seminar at Syracuse University explaining the distinction between (and possible intersecting points of) copyright and plagiarism.

Here's how I compare and contrast these two concepts: Copyright simply is a set of laws that governs the creation, reproduction, and distribution of original works that can be perceived. Copyright law is codified as a federal statute at Title 17 of U.S. Code. The most important things to remember about copyright are that 1) it is a set of laws and 2) allegations of wrongdoing—the illegal use of protected works without exception, license, or purchase—are made within the context of a standardized legal process. But more about this process later.

Plagiarism, in comparison, is the act of stealing and passing off someone else's ideas or words as one's own without crediting the source, as defined in Merriam-Webster Online. Brief or at-

Copyright vs. Plagiarism

Copyright	Plagiarism
Using someone else's creative idea, which can include a song, a video, a movie clip, a piece of visual art, a photograph, and other creative works, without authorization or compensation, if compensation is appropriate.	Using someone else's idea (usually a written idea) without giving proper credit for the idea—a failure to cite adequately.
Enforced by the courts	Enforced by the schools
Against federal law, and penalties include fines and, more recently, imprisonment. For many years, copyright was a civil offense; now it is a blend of civil and criminal offenses. Powerful lobbies, including software manufacturers and the recording and motion picture industries, have taken an active role in enforcing copyright.	Forbidden by institutional code. The penalties are failing grades or expulsion as a result of violating institutional codes. It is not addressed by our legal system in any real way, except for some scientific circumstances. It is enforced by public censure and punishments by institutions.

Taken from: "Plagiarism and Copyright—What Are the Differences?" The National Council of Teachers of English, *Council Chronicle*, November 2005.

tributed quotes generally do not constitute plagiarism. Typically, no law governs plagiarism, so no one can be sued for plagiarism. Ultimately, plagiarism is about idea theft: A person tries to take an idea and claim it as his or her own.

There is also a potential intersection between plagiarism and copyright. For example, an idea can be plagiarized, but an idea cannot be copyrighted. However, if that idea is committed to paper (or otherwise recorded), then the idea can be both plagiarized *and* infringed. So let's take this a step further: While a recorded idea can be subject to plagiarism and copyright infringement, a person could use a recorded idea if that use falls under one or more copyright exceptions. Qualifying for one of the exceptions may remove the copyright infringement risk, but it may not necessarily remove the plagiarism risk.

In fact, a person who adds some level of ironic twist to the use may be considered a parodist and make that parody his own new, unique work that is subject to its own copyright protection. Or, given our working definition of plagiarism—the act of stealing and passing off another's ideas or words as one's own without crediting the source—one could reasonably argue that the act of parody constitutes a form of plagiarism. In many parodies, the source of the parody is instantly recognized, but does instant recognition equate to attribution?

In the end, though, copyright infringement and plagiarism are distinct and separate. But it is easier now to recognize how these concepts can get twisted.

Plagiarism Allegations

Even though copyright infringement can result in financial damages or even jail time, plagiarism allegations can be much more damaging to a person's professional reputation than allegations of copyright infringement. To support this statement, let's return to the Copyright Act. The act operates in a way that excuses infringement allegations. For example, fair use under Section 107 excuses an allegation of copyright infringement. Practically speaking, a judge may look at the facts of a case and determine that a party has actually made fair use of a work. Alternatively, a judge could determine that an accused's claim of a fair use excuse is errant. (The publishing industry has been making just such an argument in its lawsuit over Google Book Search.) But in the end, copyright law allows for the possibility that allegedly illegal conduct may be excusable or defensible.

Federal copyright law (along with federal rules of evidence and civil litigation procedure) also typically places certain burdens on the accuser, including the burden of proving that an infringement occurred and that the accused is the party responsible for the infringement. Copyright law also imposes prerequisites that must be met even before an accuser makes an allegation: Pursuant to Section 411, a copyright owner cannot start a copyright infringement lawsuit unless the work at issue is registered with the Copyright Office in Washington, D.C. Given the excuses available to the accused, the procedural safeguards, and evidentiary safeguards, it is easy to see how the copyright system tries to balance the rights and reputations of the accused and the accuser.

Plagiarism allegations, however, have no such safeguards. Allegations of plagiarism do not require registration, and they do not require that the accuser prove the allegation. Plagiarism allegations do not even require that the injured party be the one who alleges wrongdoing. In most cases, third parties identify potential acts of plagiarism, make public allegations, then let the public rumor mill consider the facts. The accuser is never called upon to account for the veracity or falsity of his claim.

Plagiarism cases may involve an accuser's questionable motives. For example, the person alleging plagiarism in the Ohio University case is an alumnus who was initially unable to get his thesis topic approved, according to the *WSJ* article. The article fails to ask (or answer) what seems to be an obvious question: Did the accuser have a big enough grudge against the students who graduated before him to discredit their work? While no proof exists that the accuser in the Ohio University scandal was fueled by such a motive, it is still a legitimate question.

Further, the *WSJ* report does not identify any conclusive determination that any of the alleged plagiarizers intentionally used another person's content with the intent to deceive the reader that such content (or the ideas therein) was original. The story includes reports that seem worth investigating, but it seems the burden now lies with the accused to prove the claim effectively: They did not plagiarize. That is a tough position to be in.

What's more, plagiarism claims inherently presume that the accused has a guilty mind: The alleged plagiarist intentionally and knowingly copied and failed to attribute another person's work. But in many well-known plagiarism cases, the accused deny any intent to fail to attribute. Some say it is industrial sloppiness.

This may or may not be true, but if industrial sloppiness—not stealth—is the real reason for not attributing something, then that seems different than an instance where a person's *mens rea* is such that he meant to cheat. Certainly, the former does not seem to warrant destruction of the accused's professional reputation.

(As an aside, an issue that seems to be lost within these discussions is the failure of educational institutions—domestic and international, at all levels—to train students properly for the rigors of high-level academic work, including technical writing and citation. That subject should be addressed elsewhere.)

The lack of standards in plagiarism cases make an accusation virtually impossible to defend, but the mere allegation of plagiarism is considered an often irreversible smudge against a person's professional and personal values and ethics. This modern version of the scarlet letter points to one of the biggest problems with plagiarism: Without any clear standard, no burden of proof, and virtually no defenses, mere accusations of plagiarism can crush reputations faster than any allegation of copyright infringement.

Potential Plagiarism Solutions

This plagiarism controversy will not end any time soon. Interestingly, information professionals can play a role in helping knowledge workers with academic and technical writing. From a reference standpoint, several academic and corporate libraries will have subject matter specialists to help sift through and manage the literature on a given topic. The best librarians also will be quite familiar with standard citation conventions in that literature, and perhaps even will have available citation style guides that distill citation intricacies into manageable and repeatable steps.

Some libraries are even going further by providing access to Web-based citation management software. These service offerings are consistent with the contemporary trend of moving applications off the desktop, and instead, leveraging the Web as a computing platform. The benefit to packages such as RefWorks (www.refworks.com) is that the citations are centrally located and organized, and accessible from a reliable Web connection. Many of these packages also interface both with on-line databases and with Voyager-based library systems. This integration lets you drop citations right into the software from articles and catalog records.

Plagiarism accusations can dog and derail professional careers, even of those who have made legitimate or honest errors. The best way to stay out of plagiarism's bright, unflattering spotlight is to identify citation customs (these will differ according to industry), learn those customs and citation standards, and, where possible, seek training or assistance in mastering and applying those standards.

THREE

Plagiarism Is Increasing

Don Campbell

> Don Campbell, a writer and journalism lecturer at Emory University, wrote this article for *National CrossTalk*, a publication of the National Center for Public Policy and Higher Education. The Center is a nonprofit, independent organization that advocates for laws and public policies that will help Americans gain quality education beyond high school. The following viewpoint examines the increasing incidences of plagiarism at college campuses, citing the increased availability of written material through the Internet and the decreased emphasis on ethical values in high schools as the primary causes. Campbell also examines university responses to this plagiarism epidemic, particularly the use of honor codes and commercial antiplagiarism services.

The problem of cheating in academia hit Tom Lancaster in a very personal way more than a decade ago: The Emory University political science professor found his own research being plagiarized by one of his students. . . .

"The student," said Lancaster, "had clearly in my mind simply plagiarized a previous paper—not necessarily the words—but had simply pulled out the data." Lancaster took the case to the Emory honor council, but the council judged the student not guilty because the data had not been published. The student admitted finding it in a fraternity file.

To add insult to injury, after Lancaster gave the student an F in the course, he found out a year later that the grade was changed without his being notified. "It really was the shot across the bow for me," said Lancaster, who has been a crusader for a more stringent honor code and judicial process at Emory ever since.

Plagiarism Goes High-Tech

Today, in the era of the internet and other high-tech gadgetry, Lancaster's story seems almost quaint. Fraternity and sorority files are antiques when students can use computers, cellphones, calculators and iPods to cheat and plagiarize their way to better grades.

And the response among college administrators, faculty and students on honor councils has been inadequate, uneven and at times confused. Those who would fight fire with fire, or technology with technology, are squared off against those who want to change a culture that—beginning in high school—spawns the attitude that cheating is no big deal.

The Plagiarism Plague

What's not debatable, according to ongoing research, is that cheating and plagiarism in the country have reached epidemic proportions on college campuses.

The Center for Academic Integrity, based at Duke University, calls the latest findings from the research by Donald McCabe, a Rutgers University professor, "disturbing, provocative and challenging." McCabe has surveyed some 50,000 students on more than 60 campuses since the fall of 2002. Among his major findings, released last summer:

• On most campuses, 70 percent of students admit to some cheating, with half admitting to one or more instances of serious cheating on written assignments.

- Internet plagiarism is exploding because students are uncertain about how to properly use content from the internet, with 77 percent of those surveyed saying it is not a serious issue.
- Faculty are reluctant to take action. Some 44 percent of faculty members surveyed over the past three years who were aware of cheating in their classes did not report it.
- Academic honor codes do reduce cheating: The incidence of serious test cheating is one-third to one-half lower on campuses that have honor codes.

McCabe also found that cheating is a major problem in high school. In surveys of 18,000 high school students over the last four years, more than 70 percent of those in public or parochial schools admitted to having cheated on a test.

McCabe has been churning these figures out for many years, but is anyone taking them seriously? At the high school level, said McCabe, "I'd say they are, but boy that's not based on a lot of

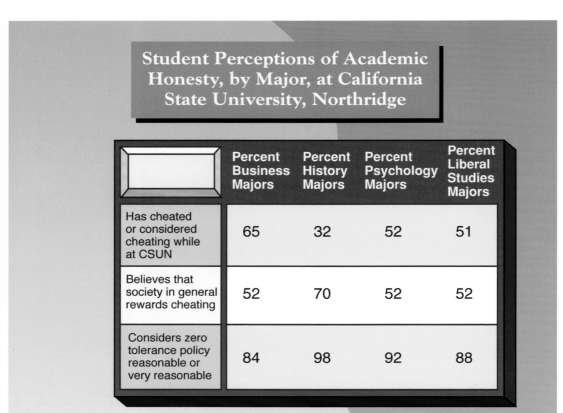

Student Perceptions of Academic Honesty, by Major, at California State University, Northridge

	Percent Business Majors	Percent History Majors	Percent Psychology Majors	Percent Liberal Studies Majors
Has cheated or considered cheating while at CSUN	65	32	52	51
Believes that society in general rewards cheating	52	70	52	52
Considers zero tolerance policy reasonable or very reasonable	84	98	92	88

Taken from: Jeremy Foster, "Cheating and Plagiarism Rampant on College Campuses," *Daily Sundial*, December 14, 2006.

data." At the college level, he said, "Some are taking it seriously enough, and some are doing a PR job, talking the right story but not fundamentally changing. Some are staying away from it because of the negative publicity that can be associated with it. Some schools I've surveyed have not had great results and they've gone public with it. I give them a lot of credit for that." . . .

Plagiarism and the Internet

The big culprit is the internet, according to researchers, higher education officials and students alike. Other kinds of technology-driven cheating occur, of course. Students may use text messaging on their cellphones to exchange test answers, or enter them on graphics calculators, or download answers or lectures on their iPods, but those methods can be dealt with by banning those devices from the classroom during tests.

The internet, however, is ubiquitous. It is a tempting venue for students looking for ideas and essays that closely parallel their assignments. In fact, online services now exist that will sell a student an essay on practically any subject imaginable. And there are also online services for faculty that will run essay excerpts through a search engine to see if they match anything available on the internet.

"Internet plagiarism is probably by far the most common form of cheating, or academic dishonesty," said Didi Kuo, a 2005 Emory graduate who chaired the university's honor council. "The main difference is that, instead of before, when you had bits and pieces of plagiarism from books and articles, when students actually went to the library, now you just get huge chunks of entire papers that come from a web source."

Renee Williams, an Emory student honor council member who previously chaired the honor council at Emory's Oxford College, believes internet plagiarism is on the rise. "It's just so easy and accessible," she said. . . .

A Cheating Culture

The problem in dealing with cheating is that it involves more than technology, it also reflects the attitudes of students and faculty, and the culture in which they coexist. High schools don't emphasize ethical values nearly enough, some experts argue, and students thus arrive at college with an attitude that it's all right to cut corners, or they simply don't understand what constitutes plagiarism.

"Getting into the best school—and seizing whatever means necessary to make that happen—seems to be valued more than the actual education," said Timothy Dodd, executive director of the Center for Academic Integrity. "Loading up on courses, majors and extra-curriculars—a quantity of involvement—has produced highly scheduled and busy young people who have to resort to shortcuts, to check everything off on their daily planner, and who have no time for reflection. Combine that with the reigning cynicism that surrounds business, politics, sports and religion, and it is no surprise that in the absence of a comprehensive focus on academic integrity, students will resort to and justify cheating as a way to get ahead in our society."

Emory graduate Kuo echoed that assessment. "At places like Emory and top-tier private universities, there is a high level of competition and a need to succeed, coupled with a privileged background," said Kuo. "So a lot of times, students have this attitude, of, you know, my father is whoever he is, and therefore I can get away with things. I'm not saying cheating is confined to these groups, but by and large, students feel that they can get away with things and that they also deserve good grades, because of the money they're paying to go here or because they worked so hard in high school."

Teachers Respond

And while faculty are the main sources of cheating complaints, some are reluctant to report cheating because they are concerned about the effect on the students, or feel that the honor code system is not efficient. Some faculty at Emory "feel the system is broken and it's not worth turning in cases," said Dean Lancaster. "Some are cynical."

Faculty may also be "all mercy and no justice," said Dodd. "They take the long view, which is, 'Will my action in some way preclude a successful future for the student?'" In general, Dodd said, students "come to the table more concerned and more aware of the extent of the problem than faculty."

If there is a broad consensus on the extent and cause of the problem, there is no consensus on how to solve it.

Honor Codes

While a growing number of colleges and universities have adopted honor code systems—no one has a precise tally of the total—their operations and range of sanctions vary widely. They routinely devote two or more hours of the orientation program for first-year students to explain the honor code, and most require students to sign a paper saying they will uphold the code.

The gold standard for honor codes is at Washington and Lee University and the University of Virginia. On those campuses, exams are not proctored, students are required to report cheating

Some research shows that incidences of plagiarism on college campuses have risen dramatically.

they observe, and students run the judicial system. And there is only one sanction if a student is found guilty—expulsion.

Other universities have adopted a "modified" honor system with a range of penalties. At the University of Maryland, for example, most students who are found responsible for academic dishonesty receive an "XF" grade which is recorded as "failure due to academic dishonesty." First-time offenders can usually have the "XF" removed from their record if they attend an academic integrity seminar.

Rutgers University's McCabe favors the "modified" approach because his research has convinced him that students are not going to turn in their classmates. "Students object to a system that tries to put an obligation on them to report," said McCabe. "There have been a number of schools in the last decade or so that tried to go to the full-fledged honor code and lost the vote at the student level on that issue. They've come back a couple of years later without the reporting requirement, and they've been successful."

Technology as a Solution

More and more schools, with and without honor codes, are opting for the technological approach to policing cheaters. This is not just a matter of students using cut-and-paste to rip off master's theses and research papers found on the web. Schools are up against a wide range of online services with names like "Term Paper Relief" and "The Paper Store" that will, for a cost of $10 to $20 a page, provide "research assistance" for students to "use as a guide" in their "own original work."

To combat this, as well as internet plagiarism generally, an online service called "Turnitin.com" has become the hottest thing on the market. It charges schools thousands of dollars a year to permit their faculty to submit essays and other student papers to be checked for plagiarism.

At the University of Iowa, for example, which spends about $11,000 a year on Turnitin, Associate Provost Lola Lopes says that anecdotal reports from faculty suggest that Turnitin has solved the plagiarism problem in their classes.

But Turnitin is controversial and has been rejected at some campuses after faculty protested that using the service routinely is unfair to students. Allitt, who wanted to see the service introduced at Emory, says the dean of the college was willing to purchase it, but that some faculty said it would be a violation of the honor code to assume that students might be violating it.

"They (faculty) want to assume that students aren't cheating —until they have overwhelming evidence to the contrary," said Allitt. "And they thought it would be an act of bad faith on our part to do that. But I certainly think it's necessary, because there's no doubt that it's going on all the time around us."

In much the same vein, discussions about using Turnitin at Washington and Lee have foundered. "Having it used on a regular basis makes the assumption that people are assumed guilty until proven innocent, rather than the other way around," said Dean of Students Dawn Watkins.

Rutgers University's Donald McCabe also opposes the regular use of plagiarism-detection programs. "If you're going to use it on everything that's submitted, you're saying to students, 'I can't trust you; I've got to check everything you do.'" McCabe said he uses Turnitin "only when I have other reasons to believe I might have a problem. In other words, I'm going to give my students the benefit of the doubt unless I see something that concerns me." . . .

Those with the broadest perspective on academic dishonesty argue that playing "gotcha" with students is not the answer— that fostering the right environment is the only long-term solution. This approach focuses heavily on stressing moral values in orientation sessions and expecting faculty to make clear to students what won't be tolerated.

At Washington and Lee, said Watkins, "We spend so much time at the front end educating our students about the process, that the fear of that single sanction—expulsion—is so great that we tend to have lower levels of self-reported cheating than most places. "Part of our known culture is that we're a place where the honor system is a key school tradition," she added. "And I think that in itself helps us in stemming the growth of cheating."

"We have to inculcate in students the habits of character," said Duke University's Dodd. "We have research that suggests that students who do not abide by the norms and standards of the academic community are more likely to violate the norms and standards of the workplace. Students need to hear consistently that academic integrity matters, and they need to understand consistently what the guidelines are as they apply in each and every class."

FOUR

The Internet Has Made Plagiarism Easier for Students

Kimberly Embleton and Doris Small Helfer

Copying papers is nothing new in schools, but the Internet has made copying much easier. Two university librarians, Kimberly Embleton and Doris Small Helfer, discuss this phenomenon in the following viewpoint. They explain the many different types of Web sites that are out there selling or giving away research papers. As well, they explain why using these services is a bad idea and offer suggestions to teachers for preventing this kind of plagiarism from happening in the first place.

Academic cheating, including buying term papers, went on long before the invention of the Internet or the World Wide Web.

There have always been students who have found ways to cheat on exams or to buy term papers from other students. The cheaters may even have purchased them from companies advertising in a local college paper or on bulletin boards around campus. Fraternity brothers or sorority sisters have sometimes shared papers. Some wealthier students have paid poorer, but brighter, students to do work for them. A glaring low-tech example occurred in the case of Wal-Mart heiress, Elizabeth Paige Laurie,

Kimberly Embleton and Doris Small Helfer, "The Plague of Plagiarism and Academic Dishonesty," *Searcher*, June 2007, pp. 23–26. www.infotoday.com/searcher. Reproduced by permission.

With ready-made term papers available for purchase on numerous Web sites, the Internet makes plagiarism as easy as pointing and clicking.

who had to return her B.A. degree in communications in 2005, when ex-roommate Elena Martinez revealed to *20/20* news magazine that Ms. Laurie had paid her $20,000 to do three term papers and numerous homework assignments.

Nonetheless, the Internet and the World Wide Web have made academic dishonesty considerably easier and faster. It is simpler than ever before to find other people's words on a topic and pass them off as your own with a simple copy-and-paste maneuver. Students often don't think their teachers can or will try to verify their work using the Internet. The Web has also made it easier to find just the right (or should we say just the *wrong*) company to use for getting term papers done for you. The options have increased vastly with the rise of the Internet. When we started looking for sources, the huge number of Web sites we found were mind boggling and, in some cases, mind-numbing! It almost makes you lose hope when you read that any type of paper you want could be purchased either off the shelf or even custom-ordered—and that even includes dissertations.

Many sites offer off-the-shelf and ready-to-go term papers. These are, of course, the cheapest ones available and, of course, the easiest ones for your professor to catch. If the professor has given the same assignment before, they may have even read this exact paper or have already identified it as a plagiarized work. Professors these days can run papers against antiplagiarism software. More difficult is catching those who can afford to buy customized term papers. While antiplagiarism software can detect what it knows about, it has a much harder time detecting what it does not know. Truly customized research papers could be difficult, if not impossible, to detect through antiplagiarism software.

That does not mean that smart faculty can't catch even those who buy customized term papers. To ensure that students actually do their own term papers, professors can ask to see the term paper outline and monitor the various steps in writing the paper along the way. A professor could require printouts of the research articles the students are using, verifying that the students have tapped content from the databases to which their school or college library subscribes.

To ensure that the students use high-quality information when writing a term paper, professors might require students to find credentials for the authors of Web sites they cite. Figuring out who authored Web content, their backgrounds, motivations, or points of view may constitute a good lesson in critical thinking in itself. Teaching students how to critique the quality of Web sites and evaluate the quality and accuracy of information will help them in their post-academic futures. Hopefully, they can develop the skills to examine Web content more critically and to avoid sites with suspect information.

At our university, a first offense at plagiarism is treated as an opportunity to educate students about how to properly cite someone else's work. When students learn that quotation marks around someone else's words and a footnote giving where you got the quotation from constitute a legitimate and essential part of the research process, they learn the on-the-level way to use the words of others to help make a point and how to avoid plagiarism: It's not plagiarism if you give the author and researcher proper credit.

Villains and Suckers

Most annoyingly, some of these term paper mill Web sites such as OtherPeople's Papers talk rather badly about libraries and research in general. Look at this promotional language: "'After wasting countless hours at libraries, bookstores, and online, I finally realized that it was easier and cheaper to have a research model provide the information I needed.'—Bob S. . . ." Well, yes, indeed, Bob S., it *is* much easier to have someone else provide the information that you need, but what have you then learned from the experience? The purpose of going to school and learning seems to have escaped Bob S.

More disconcerting, many of these Web sites claim dissertations can be done for you. Some Web sites claim that—for an additional fee, of course—all the articles that the real author used in writing the dissertation and doing the research can be sent to you. Even if true, it still seems hard to imagine how someone expects to be able to defend dissertations for which they haven't done the research or the writing, even if they take the time to read all the articles supplied by these companies.

The real horror, though, is imagining what kind of professor someone who has purchased their dissertation will make. How will they be able to write original research articles in the future to get tenure? Will they continue to have someone else write their journal articles for them? How can they teach when they do not have a deep understanding of their field? If they go to work in companies, how well will they be able to do research and write coherent reports for their bosses? And as for the lack of integrity, well. . . .

Academic Hoaxers on the Rise

Many of us talk to our students about plagiarism and incorporate warnings into our bibliographic instruction sessions. Colleges and universities have begun investing in subscriptions to iParadigm's antiplagiarism Turnitin.com service, but professors still need to remember to use it. Our institution has an agreement with Turnitin, but in talking to professors, we found that not all of them even knew about the service. While services such as Turnitin have made plagiarism more difficult for students, the number of cases of academic dishonesty is still on the rise.

Specifically, Internet plagiarism has risen. In the past, students would buy old term papers from fellow or former students. Well, that business has changed with the new millennium. The business of selling custom-written papers on the Internet is booming. And these are not your father's paper mills in which papers were passed around and recycled to many students. These are papers written to your specifications of topic, length, and number of works cited—papers that may fly under the Turnitin.com radar. Just recently, as a test, our student newspaper, *The Daily Sundial*, purchased a custom paper from one of these sites and ran it through Turnitin. The paper passed through undetected.

So how easy is it to buy a custom-written paper? Shockingly simple. With an Internet connection and a credit card, . . . you, too, could be a proud recipient of a term paper, research paper, master's thesis, or even a doctoral dissertation, including a bibliography or works cited list. You can purchase a college administration essay to help you start your student career and go right on through to law or medical school. A simple Yahoo! search using the words "Research Papers Twelfth Night" produced almost a quarter of a million results and numerous sponsored businesses. . . .

Most of the pro-plagiarism Web sites have ready-made papers available for immediate downloading, but those obviously run a greater risk of being detected. Custom-written papers, designed to meet a specific length, number of citations, format, etc., only take a few days or less for delivery. One Web site even allows you to interview different writers and choose whom you would like to write your paper. Or you may choose to have numerous writers work on your paper in order to get it done more quickly. Most sites tout that their employees are professional writers or college professors. College professors? The very ones who should be most concerned about plagiarism!

Papers can be purchased for a per-page fee; some are touted as being free, if you ignore the hefty shipping and handling fee, of course. Most prices range from $9.99 a page to $25 a page. One Web site offered custom papers written and delivered by sunrise the following day. The cost was a mere three times the usual rate of $19.95 per page, but did not specify in which time zone the sunrise would occur. So a five-page paper could set a student back a whopping $300. Delivery is often not included in the price, either. Delivery can be done by email, fax, or standard mail. Fax and email are the least expensive options for delivery, adding an additional $2 to $4 a page extra. You may also opt to have your paper delivered to you in hardcopy by FedEx for an additional $20 to $40 flat rate. So, even a paper advertised as free could cost a very large amount once everything is tallied in. After all, not all cheaters are Wal-Mart heirs. These huge fees for papers would make the service cost prohibitive for many, leaving only wealthier students as a market.

Cheating Doesn't Pay

Not only is buying online custom papers unethical, but students often find themselves getting very badly written papers. (So what did you expect? Ecommerce integrity?) One Web site we looked at promised quality "reserch" papers about "Shakesperes Twelth night" (*sic*). A student purchasing a badly written paper suffers all the usual consequences of plagiarism, but also the added consequence of a low grade. We would assume that a student paying $200 or more for a paper would hardly appreciate a failing or low grade. And there are no money-back guarantees.

All the Web pages we looked at guarantee original, custom-written papers that are not plagiarized themselves. They really go out of their way to reassure buyers that their newly written papers will not include any plagiarized material. Mostpopular-term-papers.com claims to "use a variety of plagiarism detection resources to ensure your term paper is plagiarism free and won't end up in a mass term paper database."

Many online plagiarism detection services now offer services similar to Turnitin, either free or for a fee. And not all of them are solely for the use of professors to check their students' papers. Some of these sites offer their services to the paper mill Web sites to verify that the papers being sold have not been plagiarized. One of these resources, Plagiarism Guru, announces that it is known "Worldwide as the standard in online plagiarism prevention." Another online paper mill contracts with this service, guaranteeing in a logo from Plagiarism Guru that it is "plagiarism safe." . . . In effect, the papers are not plagiarized until the student actually turns them in and claims them as his own original work.

So What Can We Do?

Teachers and librarians usually incorporate some kind of instruction or warnings about plagiarism into the class curriculum. We explain to students what constitutes plagiarism. We give them guidelines on writing citations and how to give credit where credit is due. Our institutions subscribe to Turnitin.com or other companies that can help identify previously used materials. But, as noted earlier, these custom papers could pass through plagiarism detectors with flying colors, since, technically, these papers are original works not turned in or published before. We imagine that some students might actually consider these purchased papers acceptable for those same reasons. After all, the papers were not prewritten and used before. The students didn't take them verbatim from a Web site or a journal article.

Universities really need to make it crystal clear to students that turning in any work that they did not create is plagiarism. The standard warning in a class syllabus may not be detailed enough to fully educate the students in exactly what constitutes plagiarism. Many universities have academic honor codes, but students probably get those codes along with a large package of information about the university when they are accepted or enrolled. It does not seem to make an impact on them until they are caught and threatened with expulsion. Some simply do not seem to care, as evidenced by the sharply increasing numbers who openly admit to cheating.

Detecting some plagiarism is relatively simple for many faculty. Many times faculty get suspicious if a student cannot speak well or communicate clearly in class, but yet suddenly seems able to write a perfect paragraph or page in a paper, one inconsistent with their perceived writing style or abilities. In some cases, students copy from works in the field with which the professor is very well acquainted or more shockingly even may have written themselves! Perhaps if the cheaters paid more attention in class and studying, they wouldn't make such obvious mistakes, but then they probably wouldn't be cheaters.

More and more, faculty are asking that students show their progress throughout the research process by requiring students to submit outlines, research notes, and drafts. These can demonstrate that the papers are indeed the students' own original work. Continued collaboration and work between academic faculty and their librarians can also help reduce the problem.

FIVE

The Prevalence of Plagiarism Is the Result of a Dishonest Society

Joe Saltzman

Joe Saltzman wrote this editorial article for *USA Today Magazine*. Saltzman is associate mass media editor of *USA Today* and associate dean and professor of journalism at the University of Southern California Annenberg School for Communication in Los Angeles. In the following viewpoint he argues that lying is a way of life for most Americans and supports his argument with many examples: Parents lie to their children in the name of Santa Claus and the Tooth Fairy. Despite the clear condemnation of lying found in the Bible, many clergy and church officials have been caught in financial and sex abuse cover-ups. Student writers and professional writers alike seem to have lost touch with honesty. When people in government are caught lying, it is no longer surprising, and the media, concerned about drawing an audience, accepts it. Saltzman concludes by saying that this dishonesty has corrupted the very soul of our country and challenges the news media to hold us all accountable.

Everybody lies. From the president of the U.S. to Congress to the smallest citizen in the country, we are a nation of liars. Parents still try to teach their children not to do so. They retell

Joe Saltzman, "Lying as America's Pastime," *USA Today Magazine*, July 2006, p. 25. www. usatoday.com. Copyright © 2006 Society for the Advancement of Education. Reproduced by permission.

the story of George Washington and the cherry tree or recite Proverbs 6:16–19 to make their point. Yet, with the same breath, they tell their kids, if they are not good, Santa Claus will not bring them any presents. They also urge their offspring to leave their teeth under the pillow so the Tooth Fairy will reward them. Youngsters discover at an early age that skirting the truth will keep them out of trouble: "I didn't do it; she did." "It wasn't my fault." "I don't know why the toilet overflowed. It just did."

White lies are rationalized by young and old alike as a way of being kind to people. They entail false compliments ("I love that dress on you"), lazy excuses ("I'll call you back tomorrow"), and broken promises ("I won't ever do that again"). As we grow older, the rationalizations for lying become more complex. We cheat on our income tax returns because the tax laws are corrupt. "The check is in the mail" buys some extra time in paying a late bill; besides, what is the harm? Putting on a resumé that you graduated from college when you did not seems fair because you were just a few units shy of getting a diploma before you had to quit school because you ran out of money.

Religious People Lie

One survey determined that 90% of Americans lie under certain circumstances. Others show that many of this country's citizens are extremely religious, believing in God, Satan, and a Bible that is very specific in its condemnation of lying. Yet, members of the clergy have been caught in mistruths concerning financial dealings, corrupt practices, and pedophilia (the Catholic Church hierarchy long denied such behavior even took place). Adulterers—some surveys indicate that a significant percentage of married men and women have affairs—must lie constantly, and they lie to the people they say they love the most: spouses, children, best friends, and co-workers. Our lying to each other has become a way of life.

Most of us lie out of fear or embarrassment. If our resumés are not impressive, we are afraid we will not get that job. If we are caught doing something wrong, we will be reprimanded, fired, or even sent to jail. Some rationalizations just keep growing, mak-

A Person Has to Lie or Cheat Sometimes in Order to Succeed

	Strongly Agree or Agree (percentage)		Disagree or Strongly Disagree (percentage)	
	2002	2004	2002	2004
High Schools (overall)	43	42	57	59
Public High Schools	42	42	58	58
Private Religious High Schools	42	41	58	59
Private Nonreligious High Schools	36	41	64	59
Overall High School Responses	4,777	9,418	6,397	13,261

Taken from: *Report Card 2004: The Ethics of American Youth*, Question 9, Josephson Institute's 2002 and 2004 surveys on the ethics of American youth.

ing the liar almost appear noble and kind of heart: "I don't want my wife to find out I'm having an affair because it would hurt her and the children." "I cheat on my tax return because the government is using my tax dollars to wage an unjust war that is killing innocent people." "I'm a good person and the lie really didn't hurt anybody. In fact, it saved a lot of bruised feelings."

Writers Lie

Plagiarism—passing off another's work as your own—and fabrication have become commonplace, especially in student papers at all levels of American education. Moreover, it has seeped into the media. Writers of nonfiction books and memoirs have been caught lying about past events. Staff writers on such august publications as the *New York Times* and *New Republic* have made up or improperly enhanced stories. In broadcast news, pieces are lifted out of publications without attribution or apology. Few electronic or internet news media bother checking quotes or facts that they steal from other publications. Most of the students or journalists caught red-handed seem more frustrated that they were caught than apologetic for what they have done. Some do not seem to understand that using other people's work without attribution or simply fabricating quotes and facts is dishonest. Actually, this regressive brand of journalism merely appears to be a logical extension of the dishonesty in business and personal relationships overtaking the country.

Norman Finkelstein is pictured holding a copy of his book, in which he documents the alleged plagiarism of fellow author and attorney Alan Dershowitz in Dershowitz's work The Case for Israel.

Elected Officials Lie

Lying has become such an integral part of society that no one seems outraged by it anymore, even when that lie has extraordinary and painful consequences. So, when the president or a congressman is caught in a lie, the public seems to accept it as just business as usual. It turns out that it does not really matter what the real reasons were for going to war in Iraq. The end justifies any means, any lies, any deceptions, any dishonest behavior.

The policy of government today seems to be that, if the truth is offensive, ignore it and make up a story. Global warming? It does not really exist. Results of global warming? Blame it on something else. Annoyed that science does not support your point of view? Ridicule it and make up your own explanation. If anyone in or out of government dares to tell the truth, minimize their participation in government and send them on their way.

The Media Accepts Lying

The news media appears utterly confused about the acceptance of lying as a way of life. With the exception of "The Daily Show with Jon Stewart" (which is a "fake news" organization), few media outlets ever point out a lie or deception until long after it has served their purpose. Using the excuse of balanced coverage and fairness, the press seems to give any point of view, any lie, any deception equal time with people who actually are telling the truth. Scientific fact is given equal time with anyone's point of view. Expert testimony is equated with gossip and opinion. When in doubt, the news media always falls back on old, reliable audience-pleasers like celebrity journalism, consumer news, the weather, and sports—topics that do not offend or confuse.

The problem is that private behavior and public policy built on deception corrupt the heart and soul of a country and its people, leaving both morally bankrupt and untrustworthy. The news media should be worried about this, reminding readers and viewers about this epidemic of deceit that goes from the highest office in the land to the average person on the street. They should be telling us on a daily basis that a lying tongue not only is an abomination to God, but one that is intolerable to any conscientious citizen.

SIX

Plagiarism Is the Result of Students Who Are Unwilling to Learn

Jonathan Malesic

The *Chronicle of Higher Education* is a weekly newspaper for college and university professors and administration. In the following viewpoint Jonathan Malesic, an assistant professor of theology at King's College in Wilkes-Barre, Pennsylvania, questions why students think that their professors will not notice the paragraphs that they have cut and pasted from the Internet and inserted into their papers. He concludes that since students who plagiarize do not read critically, they believe that their professors will not either. He points out that, ironically, if a student has the skills to plagiarize without detection, then the student has the skills to write the paper without cheating.

It happened more times last year than I can even recall, but I clearly remember the first time. I was grading a paper and came across a sentence that surprised me. It just didn't fit in with what I had read up to that point. I was surprised partly because the sentence made proper use of the word "implacable," whereas in the paragraph before, the student had used an abstract noun ending in "-ship" as a verb. Twice.

I read more and found more seismic shifts in the writing style. Magisterial paragraphs were followed by inane ones; syllogisms gave way to circular logic, and back again. I picked one suspect sentence, entered it into an Internet search engine, and in milliseconds, I found it—word for word, punctuation mark for punctuation mark. It turned out much of the rest of the paper had been plagiarized from the same document.

I deduced that the student had also performed a "find-and-replace" function on one key word in the document to make paragraphs that were on a different topic seem as if they were on the topic I had assigned.

Plagiarism Insults a Professor's Intelligence

Did this cheeky twerp think I wouldn't notice? For an hour after I found the paper's origin, I could only sit in my office and stew, comparing the paper to the Internet version again and again and determining that, at most, one paragraph was entirely original to the student.

My anger then turned into self-questioning. What did I do to this student to deserve such an insult? How had I failed as a teacher, to make the student think that stealing someone else's words was acceptable?

Since I was a new assistant professor, I sought my colleagues' advice about the paper. They sympathized, they shared my indignation, but as I calmed down, they also told me that I shouldn't take it personally. Apparently I would be seeing cases like this again. Senior colleagues gave matter-of-fact appraisals of just how many plagiarized papers I could expect in a given class of 25 students.

They were right. Throughout the year, I saw plagiarized papers in nearly every stack I read. At times, I started to think that maybe every paper was plagiarized.

My extreme reaction to that first plagiarized paper was partly the result of my having been unprepared for it. I had seen a case or two of cheating when I was a teaching assistant, but it didn't seem like a personal affront. After all, it wasn't my class. Cheating was the professor's problem, so I felt no need to look for explanations.

off the mark.com — by Mark Parisi

YOUR TERM PAPER ON "THE GROWING PROBLEM OF PLAGIARISM IN SOCIETY" IS EYE-OPENING...ESPECIALLY SINCE IT'S THE THIRD TIME I'VE SEEN IT...

© 2003 MARK PARISI DIST. BY UFS., INC. offthemark.com

Cartoon copyrighted by Mark Parisi, printed with permission, offthemark.com.

Plagiarists Underestimate Their Audience

There are probably dozens of reasons why some students plagiarize. They're lazy. They're afraid. They perceive plagiarism to be standard practice. They believe that any means to a good grade are legitimate.

What's most astounding, though—and most insulting—is that students plagiarize in ways that are so easy to catch. They cut and paste without thinking to cover their tracks. They copy from the most obvious sources possible. They find and replace words and then do not proofread to ensure clarity. Do they think we're stupid? If they're going to plagiarize, why can't they at least do it in a way that acknowledges that their audience is intelligent? Don't they know what the big framed diplomas on our walls mean?

I think that student plagiarists are often poor plagiarists because they don't realize that it's even possible to be a savvy reader, that it's possible to read a text that has been cobbled together from multiple sources and determine where one source's contribution ends and another's begins. Those students don't pay attention to diction, syntax, or tone when they read, so they can't possibly imagine that someone else might.

If that is, in fact, what goes on (or, rather, doesn't go on) in our students' minds when they are copying material, then we may have run into an example of a broad human tendency to take our individual selves as the standard by which we judge everyone else. The philosopher Ludwig Feuerbach noticed that tendency, explaining the difference between two bad poets like this: "He who, having written a bad poem, knows it to be bad, is in his intelligence, and therefore in his nature, not so limited as he who, having written a bad poem, admires it and thinks it good."

Students Need Examples of Good Work

If Feuerbach is right, then by showing our students what good work is, helping them discover what makes it good work, and explaining how we can very clearly tell the difference between good and bad work, or the relative differences between two authors, we are not only improving their minds, but improving their "natures." That is a lofty word, one that even humanities professors (maybe especially humanities professors) hesitate to utter. But maybe we can agree at least that we can try to broaden students' perspectives and raise their standards, so that they can be better critics—and better self-critics.

Students can't entirely be blamed for the narrow-mindedness they come to college with, but they absolutely can be blamed for persisting in it in the face of their colleges' best efforts to expand their horizons. Plagiarism is, therefore, not only dishonest; it is also a sign of students' shamefully entrenched satisfaction with their limitations.

I no longer see cases of blatant plagiarism as personal insults. They are, instead, the pathetic bleats of students who think they know enough—maybe all there really is to know—about how to read and think and write.

The paradox of plagiarism is that in order to be really good at it, you need precisely the reading and writing skills that ought

Easy-to-use search engines help students find a plethora of information on the Web. Avoiding plagiarism, however, requires learning proper research techniques, such as checking the authority of Web sites and properly citing sources.

to render plagiarism unnecessary. If my students could recognize what differentiates their own writing styles from those of authors whose work they find online, then they should also be able to perform with ease all the tasks I require for their essay assignments: to read texts carefully, to determine the relative importance of textual evidence, to formulate a clear thesis, and to defend it convincingly.

I'll grant that my hypothesis that students plagiarize so obviously because they are unable to imagine someone noticing does not cover all cases. I have caught even students whose other work and class participation exhibit exactly the skills that ought to obviate the perceived need to plagiarize. Maybe I should be insulted by those students: They know better and still try to fool me.

I believe in relentlessly exercising my students' critical abilities, but I also believe in punishing plagiarism. A student who plagiarizes refuses to be educated. There shouldn't be room in my classroom for that kind of student. Indeed, that person is not really a student at all.

SEVEN

Plagiarism Is Difficult to Avoid

Joseph Epstein

The line between plagiarism and original work can be very clear, but it can also be very fuzzy. In the following viewpoint Joseph Epstein describes a recent incident in which an unidentified writer blatantly plagiarized from an earlier essay that Epstein wrote for the *Weekly Standard*. Epstein also lists many famous and respected writers who have been accused of plagiarism and reflects on his own fear of unintentionally plagiarizing. Epstein is a noted writer, and his essays appear in the Best American Essays series. He also was a distinguished lecturer at Northwestern University in Chicago, Illinois. Most recently, he is a contributing editor at the *Weekly Standard*.

If imitation is the sincerest form of flattery, what is plagiarism? The least sincere form? A genuine crime? Or merely the work of someone with less-than-complete mastery of quotation marks who is in too great a hurry to come up with words and ideas of his own?

Over many decades of scribbling, I have on a few occasions been told that some writer, even less original than I, had lifted a phrase or an idea of mine without attribution. I generally took this as a mild compliment. Now, though, at long last, someone has plagiarized me, straight out and without doubt. The theft is from an article of mine about Max Beerbohm, the English comic writer. . . .

The man did it from a great distance—from India, in fact, in a publication calling itself "India's Number One English Hindi news source;" the name of the plagiarist is being withheld to protect the guilty. I learned about it from an email sent to me by a generous reader.

Here is the plagiary:

JE [Joseph Epstein]: "Beerbohm was primarily and always an ironist, a comedian, an amused observer standing on the sidelines with a smile and a glass of wine in his hand. G.K. Chesterton

Plagiarism Severity Matrix

Taken from: Erick Howenstine, "Plagiarism Page," Northeastern Illinois University Web site.

said of him that 'he does not indulge in the base idolatry of believing in himself.'"

TP (Tasteful Plagiarist): "Beerbohm was primarily and always an ironist, a comedian, an amused observer standing on the sidelines with a smile and a glass of wine in his hand. G.K. Chesterton rightly observed of him that 'he does not indulge in the base idolatry of believing in himself.'"

In 30 years of teaching university students I never encountered a case of plagiarism, or even one that I suspected. Teachers I've known who have caught students in this sad act report that the capture gives one an odd sense of power. The power derives from the authority that resides behind the word "gotcha." This is followed by that awful moment—a veritable sadist's Mardi Gras—when one calls the student into one's office and points out the odd coincidence that he seems to have written about existentialism in precisely the same words [French existential philosopher] Jean-Paul Sartre used 52 years earlier.

Famous Plagiarists

In recent years, of course, plagiarisms have been claimed of a number of authors themselves famous enough to be plagiarized from. The historians Stephen Ambrose and Doris Kearns Goodwin were both caught in the act. The Harvard law professor Laurence Tribe has been accused of the crime. The novelist Jerzy Kosinski, a man who in some ways specialized in deceit, deposited chunks of writing from Polish sources into his books without attribution. Some years ago there was talk of plagiarism in Martin Luther King Jr.'s doctoral dissertation. Schadenfreudians [people finding pleasure in the misfortunes of others] are usually much pleased by the exposure of plagiarism in relatively high places; to discover that the mighty have not fallen so much as cheated on their way up excites many who have never attempted the climb.

Everyone Borrows

I have myself always been terrified of plagiarism—of being accused of it, that is. Every writer is a thief, though some of us are

The prevalence of information quickly accessible on the Web makes copying easy and tempting.

more clever than others at disguising our robberies. The reason writers are such slow readers is that we are ceaselessly searching for things we can steal and then pass off as our own: a natty bit of syntax, a seamless transition, a metaphor that jumps to its target like an arrow shot from an aluminum crossbow.

In my own case, I have written a few books built to a great extent on other writers' books. Where the blurry line between a paraphrase and a lift is drawn—not always so clear when composing such books—has always been worrisome to me. True, I've never said directly that man is a political animal, or that those who cannot remember the past are condemned to repeat it [both famous phrases]. Still, I worry that I may somewhere have crossed that blurry line.

It Is Better to Lend than Borrow

In the realm of plagiarism, my view is, better a lender than a borrower be. (You can quote me on that.) The man who reported the plagiarism to me noted that he wrote to the plagiarist about it but had no response. At first I thought I might write to him myself, remarking that I much enjoyed his piece on Max Beerbohm and wondering where he found that perfectly apposite G.K. Chesterton quotation. Or I could directly accuse him, in my best high moral dudgeon, of stealing my words and then close by writing—no attribution here to Rudyard Kipling, of course—"Gunga Din, I'm a better man than you." Or I could turn the case over, on a contingency basis, to a hungry young Indian lawyer, and watch him fight it out in the courts of Bombay or Calcutta, which is likely to produce a story that would make *Bleak House* look like *Goodnight Moon*.

EIGHT

Schools Use Strict Policies to Prevent Plagiarism

Scott Olsen

High schools and universities are looking for effective means to address the increased prevalence of plagiarism in their institutions. While the Internet and computer technology may tempt students to present the work of others as their own, shifting attitudes toward plagiarism among young people play a role in this increase as well. In the following viewpoint Scott Olsen, a staff writer for the *Indianapolis Business Journal*, shows readers how high schools and universities are addressing plagiarism. School conduct codes are addressing the issue head-on, especially plagiarism via the Internet. Punishments for violations are being made more severe. Educators are even using the Internet to find plagiarism from the Internet. Some see bringing students into the process of reworking conduct codes and determining punishments as a way to discourage plagiarism "from the bottom up." By changing the way students see and understand the issue, some educators hope to prevent plagiarism from happening in the first place.

Cheaters beware. High schools and universities are turning up the heat on students who pilfer information for research papers or book reports.

The term plagiarism originated from the Latin word *plagiarius*, which means kidnapper, and has existed for centuries. But the creation of the Internet has made it much easier to lift published material without crediting the source. With a few clicks of the mouse, students simply can "cut and paste" the information they need. Or, for a fee, they can purchase entire term papers online from hundreds of Web sites offering an array of topics.

Now, educational administrators are beginning to recognize the prevalence of the problem and are fighting back. Many are bolstering their rules of conduct to provide them additional disciplinary power when handing out a failing grade might not be enough.

"We began to address it about two years ago," said Stephen Heck, executive director of the Indiana Association of School Principals. "It's a whole new area. The idea of Internet plagia-

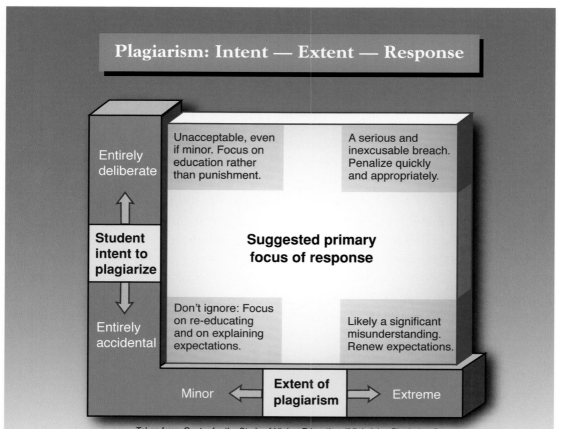

Plagiarism: Intent — Extent — Response

Entirely deliberate

Unacceptable, even if minor. Focus on education rather than punishment.

A serious and inexcusable breach. Penalize quickly and appropriately.

Student intent to plagiarize

Suggested primary focus of response

Entirely accidental

Don't ignore: Focus on re-educating and on explaining expectations.

Likely a significant misunderstanding. Renew expectations.

Minor ← **Extent of plagiarism** → Extreme

Taken from: Center for the Study of Higher Education, "Minimising Plagiarism." *Assessing Learning in Australian Universities*, 2002.

rism had never really surfaced in our schools, and now it has become a serious issue."

Many Students Think Plagiarism Is Okay

Recent studies conducted jointly by Rutgers University and the Center for Academic Integrity at Duke University shed light on the growing problem. A 2003 survey found 38 percent of more than 18,000 college students had copied material from the Internet without citing the source. The amount represented a dramatic increase from the 10 percent who admitted guilt in a similar survey just two years before. The numbers are even more striking at the high school level, in which roughly 58 percent of nearly 18,000 students said they had partaken in the practice.

Donald McCabe, a Rutgers management professor who led the studies, said the students' lack of remorse surprised him more than the numbers. In the latest survey of college students, 44 percent of those who said they had plagiarized dismissed the practice as "trivial" or "not cheating at all."

"They convince themselves that they're doing nothing wrong," he said. "That's the scary thing, because that's the attitude they're going to take out into the real world."

Universities Crack Down on Plagiarism

To help combat the problem, educators are revamping their rules of conduct or honor codes that govern student activities. At Indiana University [IU] in Bloomington, for instance, administrators are revising the student code this year [2005] to include more language specifically targeting Internet plagiarism.

Students accused of plagiarizing could receive a failing grade on the assignment, or worse, for the course, said Dick McKaig, IU's dean of students. If a pattern of violations exists, suspension or expulsion could be warranted.

In the 2003–2004 school year, faculty reported 121 cases of plagiarism, down from 150 the previous school year, McKaig said. Considering 38,000 students attend the university, the numbers hardly represent a crisis. But faculty members are not taking any chances.

Using the Internet to Combat Internet Plagiarism

They voted to renew an agreement with Turnitin.com, a California-based company that compares research papers to works in databases containing material from places students would likely go to cheat. The company flags papers with work taken from other sources. More than 5,000 schools, colleges and other institutions pay 75 cents per student for the analysis, according to the company.

"The decision to continue to participate is sort of reflective that faculty realize this is a problem that has to be addressed in forthright ways," McKaig said.

Changing a School's Culture to Discourage Plagiarism

The University of Notre Dame at South Bend is taking note, too, according to an April [2005] story in the student newspaper, the *Observer*. Committees of students, faculty and administrators last fall crafted a series of amendments to the school's honor code.

One of those approved recently by the Academic Council allows faculty to penalize students they believe have cheated, such as giving them a zero for the assignment. The punishment is a swifter option to a drawn-out departmental committee hearing, although students can still choose to argue their cases.

High School Students Are Not Off the Hook

At the high school level, school districts generally revisit their student handbooks at the end of the academic year to consider revisions. Many of those this year [2005] are including honor-code provisions in their roles of conduct that give administrators the ability to treat plagiarism as a disciplinary matter, said Jon Bailey, a partner at the locally based law firm of Bose McKinney & Evans LLP. "In situations where a bad grade wasn't enough," he said, "they wanted the ability to go a little further."

Speaking through an Indianapolis Public Schools [IPS] spokeswoman, Willie Giles, assistant superintendent of curriculum and instruction at IPS, said he thinks the issue is less of a concern

Teacher Susan Oblinger of Centerville High School in Chantilly, Virginia, monitors her students during an algebra test. Schools are giving teachers stronger ammunition to fight plagiarism.

among the K–12 ranks than at the collegiate level. He said IPS schools have no rules directly addressing online plagiarism.

Bailey estimated that roughly 10 to 15 of the school districts he represents are toughening their rules of conduct. He declined to name those districts, citing privacy matters.

Are Parents a Part of the Problem?

After conducting research about online plagiarism, Bailey said he was surprised that, in at least some cases, parents must know their students are turning in other people's works. That's because numerous Web sites offering term papers for sale require a credit card, something most high-school students don't have.

The Business Side of Plagiarism

For procrastinators, many of the sites known as "digital term paper mills" offer urgent service. At least one charges $26.95 per page instead of its standard $12.95 for delivery within 48 hours.

A plethora of topics are available from other Web sites, including such hot-button issues as abortion, cloning and U.S. foreign policy. And other sites sell customized papers to thwart plagiarism-detection software. Some actually guarantee teacher approval.

Stopping Plagiarism Before It Happens

Tim Dodd, executive director at Duke's Center for Academic Integrity, which assisted Rutgers in the studies, credited school districts for recognizing the depth of the problem. But he said they really need to be more proactive, instead of reactive, when attempting to combat cheating.

"It requires a much more comprehensive approach," Dodd said. "Schools are recognizing that they have to re-evaluate their stance on academic integrity and they have to develop the appropriate savvy to make learning valuable to students, and not subject to cheating."

NINE

Emphasizing Personal Integrity Will Prevent Plagiarism

John F. Kavanaugh

In the following viewpoint John F. Kavanaugh, a Jesuit priest and professor of ethics, social philosophy, philosophy of psychology, and philosophy of religion at St. Louis University, takes the issue of plagiarism and academic honesty in a direction that one might not expect from a university professor and priest. Kavanaugh thinks it should not be a surprise to see plagiarism and cheating increasing among students; rather, it is almost inevitable. Although we live in a society that says that it values honesty, the dishonest words and actions of many "respectable" kinds of people are seen and heard in the news. Cheating is commonplace, and so students naturally wonder why they ought to be honest in their academic life. Kavanaugh proposes that all professors, instructors, and teachers spend some classroom time discussing cheating and plagiarism because the solution to these kinds of problems is personal integrity, not stricter academic policies.

Recently I presented a short reflection on academic integrity to some faculty members at Saint Louis University. One of the reasons I was asked to do this may have been my efforts to encourage all teachers of core curriculum courses to spend some

Journalism professor Chris Hanson, right, discusses ethics in journalism during a class at the University of Maryland. Following numerous cases of media plagiarism, university journalism programs are taking a close look at the role they play in instilling professional ethics in young journalists.

time, possibly even a whole class session, on the problem of cheating—whether by plagiarism, fudging scientific findings or just copying on exams.

A report released in 2002 by the Josephson Institute of Ethics reported data from a survey of 12,000 high school students that indicated 74 percent of them had cheated on an exam at least once during the previous year. This was a jump of 13 percent over 10 years, 3 percent over just the previous two. There were similar troubling figures about stealing and lying, which led Michael Josephson, the president of the institute, to suggest that cheating had become something of a national norm.

Students, in fact all of us, realize that cheating, if found out, usually guarantees some punishment. What is often not realized is why dishonesty is ethically wrong. Why not lie?

The Dishonesty of Daily Life Breeds Academic Dishonesty

A case can be made that the moral atmosphere in which we all live and breathe is, in stark and maybe extreme terms, a culture of cheaters. Although most professions and trades, we may hope, are made up of honest people, think of the cast of characters that often dominates our news. Politicians, C.E.O.'s, accountants, lawyers, priests, students and, yes, presidents, too.

The last president [Bill Clinton] was impeached for lying under oath. The present president [George W. Bush] is accused by some of having lied us into a war. The partisans of the previous president, those who for the most part now condemn the present president, then said, "What's the big deal?" Those who detested Clinton's deception now see not a whit of it in Bush. The few who do, say: "What's the big deal? Even if the evidence wasn't there, the results were good." Ah, the joys of selective moral outrage.

And that is the second part of our problem. The human tendency to exempt one's own party, one's nation and oneself from moral standards accompanies every ethical infidelity. In the United States, however, supported as we are by an ethos whose moral mottos are "my liberty," "my choice," "my happiness," "my way works," moral exceptionalism is commonplace. Weapons of mass destruction, for example, are decried by our president as the bane of the world—except for us. It is hard for us to understand why other nations might think we are lying, or at least posturing. But from their point of view, we not only possess more W.M.D. than all the other nations of the world combined; we have actually used them to kill tens of thousands of civilians.

Cheaters Cheat Themselves

In a classroom, one cheats, of course, for a good reason. If I get away with it, I might feel like a success. But all I've got away with is learning nothing while paying tuition for it. I have suc-ceeded only in being a fraud.

Even by the utilitarian calculation so prevalent in the United States, while the short-range results of deception may, if unde-tected, seem appealing, the long-range negative consequences are devastating. Lies inevitably erode one's own self-respect as well as trust in relationships. They also eat at the trust required for any profession and for society itself. What have Enron and Arthur Andersen done for investment and accounting? What has the Jayson Blair episode done for journalism and the *New York Times*? What have the deceptions of famous historians done for historians and the academy? As for deceptive politics, that only generates a society made up largely of uninvolved cynics on the one hand and conspiracy theorists on the other.

So far, these are arguments from bad consequences. But possi-bly the best case for honesty, even academic honesty, may rest on a form of virtue ethics. This is related to two questions:

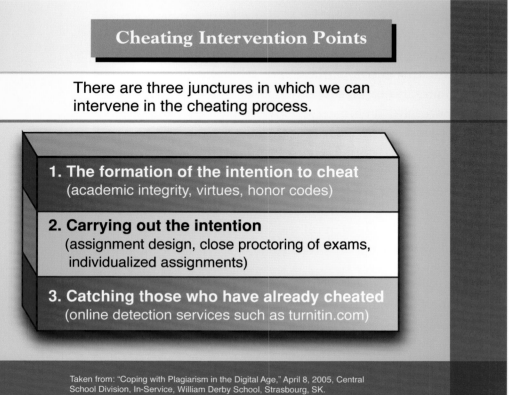

Cheating Intervention Points

There are three junctures in which we can intervene in the cheating process.

1. **The formation of the intention to cheat**
   (academic integrity, virtues, honor codes)

2. **Carrying out the intention**
   (assignment design, close proctoring of exams, individualized assignments)

3. **Catching those who have already cheated**
   (online detection services such as turnitin.com)

Taken from: "Coping with Plagiarism in the Digital Age," April 8, 2005, Central School Division, In-Service, William Derby School, Strasbourg, SK.

Whom do you admire? What kind of person do you want to be? Put negatively, the question is, what kind of behavior makes you feel small and ashamed? Usually it is some form of inauthenticity. It is when you feel like a fake, a fraud.

That is what a cheater is. And even small deceptions unfold into a way of life, of pretending, of looking good, of dreading the truth. In every consequent deception, I become the kind of person I am now choosing. Possibly all of us confront fraudulence in our lives. I know I do, and I know when I have succumbed.

Personal Integrity Effectively Combats Plagiarism

But I have also seen, at least in others, how an integrated authenticity ennobles a person. It is a sense of wholeness where we do not repress the moral impulse, where ethical passion inhabits every arena of our lives: the classroom, the boardroom, the bedroom, the War Room.

A commitment to honesty, even in small things, yields a growing knowledge of one's true self. Only on the basis of that truth can one be loved—not only by oneself, but by anyone else. The reason so many people complain of not feeling loved is that they let so few others, or even themselves, know their truth.

When those of us who are teachers show our students that we genuinely care about such things, perhaps that care itself helps them, encourages them to become the kind of persons they most deeply want to be. If this were the way we lived our personal and political lives, it might also make our families and our nation into something they often can only pretend to be.

TEN

Antiplagiarism Services Make Plagiarism Easier to Detect

Tom Warger

Tom Warger, an information technology consultant and writer, wrote this article for *University Business*, a magazine for college and university administrators. In the following viewpoint he notes that book authors, journalists, and university students recently have been under fire for frequent plagiarizing, with an increase in copying being attributed to the convenience of the Internet. He then reviews a number of antiplagiarism tools available to schools with fees ranging from hundreds to thousands of dollars. Warger also reviews some of the many plagiarism awareness-raising Web sites that are cropping up on university sites. He concludes by saying that while we will never know if plagiarism is actually more prevalent now or if it is just more detectable with new technology, the new tools being developed will likely change the face of scholarship.

The fall semester opened this year [2005] with unprecedented concern over the scope of plagiarism in higher education. A virtual epidemic of cheating, or perhaps just a new awareness, has spread across the academic world. A web search for "plagiarism" reveals numerous articles published this past summer alone in the higher education press.

Reports of book authors and journalists caught copying the works of others without attribution are also frequent. A common thread through these events is the idea that the web and internet make cheating easy. Yet many of these instances of plagiarism are detected by sharp-eyed users of the networks.

Estimates of the frequency of plagiarism by students vary, with rates of 70 percent or more often asserted. The Center for Academic Integrity at Duke University (N.C.), for example, surveyed more than 50,000 students and found that 40 percent admitted using at least a few unacknowledged borrowings in their papers.

Most observers concede that plagiarism is not new but wonder really how widespread it has become. The temptation to cut and paste is undeniable; the vastness of the web and internet gives an illusion of safety from detection.

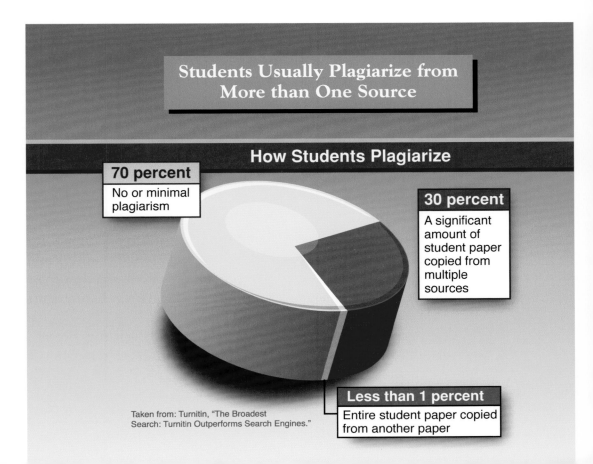

Students Usually Plagiarize from More than One Source

How Students Plagiarize

70 percent
No or minimal plagiarism

30 percent
A significant amount of student paper copied from multiple sources

Less than 1 percent
Entire student paper copied from another paper

Taken from: Turnitin, "The Broadest Search: Turnitin Outperforms Search Engines."

Cheaters exhibit varying degrees of deception. Some, desperate in the face of deadlines or simply lazy, lift a few sentences, weaving them into their own writing. Or perhaps they appropriate whole passages from sources they think nobody else will find. But others make more deliberate efforts to cover their tracks, substituting synonyms or embroidering new sentences to alter copied paragraphs.

Plagiarism-Detecting Tools

Commonly used web search engines are an obvious and easily available means for trying to counter plagiarism. If casual or incautious copiers find materials in places discoverable by ordinary searching, then faculty should be able to trace suspicious wording by the same means. But a growing multitude of software packages and search services is springing up to offer help in detecting plagiarism.

The University of Virginia website, for one, offers a free program called Wcopyfind that compares submitted files to search for shared phrases. It searches files on local and locally networked drives but is not able to search the web or internet.

The Essay Verification Engine, or EVE2, searches the web to find pages from which a writer might have plagiarized and returns links to the suspected sites, highlighting in red all the passages in the submitted paper that appear to have been copied from the detected sources. Compatible with Microsoft Word, Corel WordPerfect, or plain text formats, EVE2 sells for $30, with no recurring fees.

Plagiarism-Finder from Mediaphor Software AG, meanwhile, conducts web searches starting from texts in several formats, including Adobe PDF. The publisher suggests that authors and journalists could also use the program to check whether their texts are being plagiarized on the web. Plagiarism-Finder costs $125 and is available for a free 30-day trial.

A different approach is taken by the Glatt Plagiarism Screening Program. This program challenges writers to recreate the texts they claim to have created. It masks every fifth word of a submitted text and then measures accuracy and elapsed time while the author of that paper is challenged to fill in the blanks correctly.

The software is based on a principle that every writer has a unique style and will be highly successful at remembering written passages, even those with missing words. The Glatt Plagiarism Screening Program sells for $250.

Considered by many to be the leading anti-plagiarism product, Turnitin searches the web and some proprietary databases and a collection of already-submitted papers. A product of iParadigms, Turnitin creates what the company terms a "fingerprint" of a submitted paper, which it then compares to its three sources of information. Patterns, distributions, and profiles of language use are computed statistically and combined to yield ratings of probability of plagiarism.

Additionally, each paper submitted for testing is added to the company's database, augmenting the stock of existing papers available for each new search. Turnitin is available for campus licenses, with pricing based on institutional enrollment.

Within the past month [September 2005], iParadigms has teamed with LexisNexis to offer a new service called Copy-Guard. It searches more than six billion documents within the LexisNexis collection, using pattern-matching techniques to identify possible sources for submitted texts. While the service was not designed specifically with higher ed use in mind, it could certainly be used at schools.

Software programs and online services vary in their claims of certainty about identification of plagiarism. Some herald the end of stolen texts, while others are careful to say they report degrees of probability. But all represent themselves as tools of detection and offer themselves as specialized means to combat the epidemic of plagiarism.

Preventive Actions

Many institutions of higher education have established websites to promote student awareness of the dangers of plagiarism and ways to avoid the practice. The Student Judicial Affairs Office of the University of California, Davis has a web page entitled

John Zakarian, vice president and editorial page editor at the Hartford Courant, *is pictured in his office. The* Courant *is among a growing number of newspapers, law firms, and other businesses using antiplagiarism tools that can cross-check billions of digital documents and recognize patterns in just seconds.*

"Avoiding Plagiarism: Mastering the Art of Scholarship." It gives guidelines on how to cite sources, as well as guidelines—with examples—for avoiding inadvertent plagiarism. The site recommends Diana Hacker's *A Writer's Reference* as an authority on proper references.

A comparable web resource at Indiana University, "Plagiarism: What It is and How to Recognize and Avoid It" illustrates acceptable and unacceptable paraphrases and advises on strategy and mechanics to avoid plagiarism.

The Writing Center of Claremont McKenna College (Calif.) has published a study of software designed to teach students about the dangers of plagiarism. Students were surveyed on their assessments of the effectiveness of six software tools. Their findings were that while some of the tested products rated better than others, none were better than "marginally acceptable."

A web page at the University of Michigan gives instructors background and pedagogical advice for preventing plagiarism in their assignments and cheating on tests. Various articles and letters from faculty seek to explain why students plagiarize and what faculty can do to lessen the likelihood that work they assign will result in infractions.

General awareness-raising is widely suggested as a counter to the lure of improper copying. The most frequently suggested ways to discourage plagiarism through pedagogical adjustments are for faculty to: give unique assignments (topics not likely to be represented in the universe of papers offered for sale); assign some specific sources students must use; and require students to submit outlines, project plans, or drafts in advance of the final product. Faculty are also commonly urged to be alert for anomalies in style, format, diction, and voice in student papers—as those might be signs that passages have been plagiarized.

While no one is able to say with certainty whether plagiarism is more rampant than in the past or just more detectable now, scholarship and publication are undergoing a crisis of credibility.

Students are not alone in being implicated in improper appropriation of the work of others: Journalists and scholars have been tainted also. To some extent, faculty and editors have had to scramble to become familiar with the means for testing suspicious passages as students and writers have gotten ahead of them.

A new market for aids to search out evidence of plagiarism is developing. These tools just might join the array of reference resources that shape the conduct of scholarship and policing of intellectual property.

ELEVEN

Most Plagiarism Is Not Easy to Detect

Michael Thompson

> The following viewpoint, an essay from the *Chronicle of Higher Education*, is written under the pseudonym Michael Thompson, as the author wishes to remain anonymous. A PhD student and graduate teaching assistant chronicles his own plagiarism experience. Exhausted and disillusioned, he patched together his own ideas and ideas from scholars, written in his native language, to form a large portion of an important chapter of his doctoral dissertation. He was careful to put the material into his own words, but he copied the ideas and structure and knew that it was plagiarism. His advisers did not suspect anything; however, in the end he decided not to use his plagiarized work because it was inferior to his own work. In the essay, he also reflects upon his reasons for plagiarizing and examines how he rationalized it.

It is an unfortunate fact that many students, even good ones, plagiarize or are seriously tempted to do so at some point in their studies. Plagiarism is one of the most common forms of cheating. I know about it through my work as a teaching assistant [TA], but I also know about it firsthand. I have plagiarized without being caught.

Although we do our best to ignore it, the elephant in the middle of our academic room is this: Very few of the students who plagiarize are ever caught. It is comparatively easy to catch the ones who cheat in obvious or unsophisticated ways. Academics are aware of the usual methods plagiarists employ, like cutting and pasting parts of papers from the Internet, presenting material from published academic works as their own, and copying from each other's essays. With the growth of so-called research-writing firms online, it seems the problem is set to expand.

As a teaching assistant, I have on several occasions encountered obviously plagiarized materials, and I have always tried my

In some cases, instructors may not have the tools or the time to investigate possible instances of plagiarism, which allows it to go undetected.

best to deal fairly with the students involved. My suspicions were always based on a mismatch between a particular student's earlier work and uncharacteristically advanced arguments in a new submission. One former student told me, long after I ceased to be her TA, that she had plagiarized in my course without my noticing; I'm sure that many others have done the same.

Getting Away with Plagiarism

Roughly a year ago I plagiarized, too. I am completing a doctoral dissertation on an interdisciplinary topic that touches both the humanities and the social sciences. My material is open to a wide variety of interpretative and analytic perspectives, and my research would be defined as qualitative in nature. For the issues that I work on, there is very little original material published in English, but a good deal in a foreign—and somewhat esoteric—language in which I am fluent. Likewise, the English-speaking world contains very few experts in the field, which greatly aided my deception.

Essentially, I cut and pasted together a number of insights and ideas from several authors writing in the foreign language, combined them with some of my own work, and handed them in to my supervisors as a significant part of a draft chapter for my dissertation. One supervisor liked it, one didn't, and one didn't have time to read it. In the end I decided not to use the material, for reasons I will explain.

My plagiarism went undetected not just because the work I copied was taken from foreign-language sources. I put a good deal of effort into my fraud. I was very systematic in my use of the material—I never copied any unique idea or used any concept word for word. Rather I replicated the structure, ideas, and tone of the academics I stole from. I completely changed the language, varied the emphasis, and altered the conclusions. In truth, the plagiarized end product was a very sophisticated transformation of other people's work. When I submitted the plagiarized chapter, I told myself that it had in fact taken on some of the qualities of a postmodern pastiche [hodge-podge], an idea that I now regard as self-justification. In truth, I had submitted a forgery.

Some cases of plagiarism are difficult, perhaps impossible, to identify. With a moderate amount of preparation, work, and foresight, it is not hard for a knowledgeable academic to cheat effectively, even if—as was the case with me—the reviewers are widely published and highly regarded experts in the field. That is an unpleasant conclusion, but it seems unavoidable. If a student is well regarded by his peers and professors and perceived as bright and hard-working—as I was—then it is even easier to cheat. Very few professors have the time to hunt down work that they find only mildly suspicious, and very few academic departments own or regularly use the software that makes cheating easier to catch.

I have spent some time reflecting on why I cheated. Some of my reasons were quite banal, others more abstract, but each was related to conditions of life that many graduate students would find all too familiar.

Practical Roots of Plagiarism

One of the main reasons that I even considered plagiarizing was that I was exhausted from juggling my numerous responsibilities. My advisers were demanding work from me, and I was too tired to produce it. Besides writing up my dissertation, I was working as a teaching assistant (for embarrassingly little money), working at a second (and better-paid) job as an editor for a technology company, preparing presentations for academic seminars and conferences (an unpaid, but necessary, part of graduate-student life), and writing a paper to be submitted to a peer-reviewed journal.

And like many crimes, mine had some economic roots. My university does not give me a stipend that covers nearly all of my educational expenses, and I live in an extremely expensive city.

Emotional Roots of Plagiarism

Moreover, I was overcome at the time with cynicism about academe. My fellow graduate students seemed to be largely concerned with the number of chapters produced, names dropped, and job interviews received. Very few of our research seminars

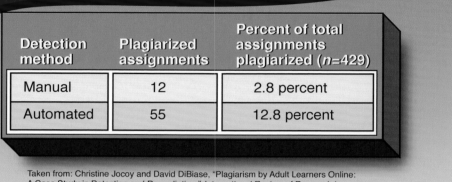

Manual vs. Automated Detection Methods

In a 2006 study, researchers found that plagiarism by online learners was more frequently detected by Turnitin services than manually by graders.

Detection method	Plagiarized assignments	Percent of total assignments plagiarized ($n=429$)
Manual	12	2.8 percent
Automated	55	12.8 percent

Taken from: Christine Jocoy and David DiBiase, "Plagiarism by Adult Learners Online: A Case Study in Detection and Remediation," *International Review of Research in Open and Distance Learning*, June 2006.

were especially inspired, and when people commented on each other's work, it seemed to be chiefly as a pretext for hearing their own voices. The idea seemed to be: Finish your dissertation as soon as you can, get out into the job market, produce articles and books, get tenured at a Great Institution, be famous, have a Festschrift published for you [a collection of essays written in honor of a scholar], and die. Except that getting tenure at Harvard replaced buying a second SUV, it seemed to be just another version of the traditional rat race.

On a more existential level, during the year of my plagiarism I was overcome by what I have come to realize was a feeling of hopelessness. My work was proceeding slowly, and I was coming to doubt my ability to attain the academic job that was the reason I had gone to graduate school.

Philosophic Rationalizations

But there were other, deeper problems. The culture at large seemed pretty grim. Did it really reward integrity? Did the social institutions that we once considered sacrosanct still value honesty, hard work, fair play? Were politicians not manipulating the truth to persuade voters to support spurious causes, like unnecessary and poorly planned wars? Were business leaders, the mass media, or the clergy any better? It might seem like avoiding responsibility to blame my plagiarism on society, but we all take our cues about what is right or wrong from the people at the top of our worlds.

Sometimes it seems that a strict code of honesty is a bit outdated. A double standard also begins to look inevitable: The stronger are often able to get away with certain things, like cheating, while the weaker tend not to. Nonetheless, I do not seek to excuse myself on the ground that I live in an imperfect world. To do so would make a mockery of all the people who have to cope with the same conditions, or worse, and yet every day attempt to live honestly and decently.

Hard Work and Poor Results

Eventually I decided to scrap my plagiarized chapter. The amount of work it had taken me to fashion a well-crafted piece of plagiarized text was only marginally less than the amount of work involved in putting together something of my own that was at least as good.

Besides, one of my supervisors thought the plagiarized piece was some of "my" weakest work. It was encouraging to believe that I could actually do a better job with the same material. After all, my name was going to be associated with the final dissertation, and thus I wanted it to be excellent and to know it was my own. I have put a significant amount of time, effort, and money into my education—why would I want my writing to be associated with mediocrity?

And here is the final point: I made a serious mistake, true enough. But I scrutinized my motives, reasoned my way through my actions, and eventually found my way to a good conclusion. You could say that all of the years I've spent acquiring a sense of liberal values came to something after all.

TWELVE

Antiplagiarism Services Violate Students' Rights

Erik W. Robelen

Many educators and students agree that plagiarism is an issue that needs addressing. In an effort to confront plagiarism head-on, some schools have employed the services of Internet-based companies that scan student papers for possible plagiarism. In the following viewpoint Erik W. Robelen, an editor for the journal *Education Week*, presents readers with one such company, Turnitin.com, and how high school students from Virginia are suing Turnitin.com for alleged copyright infringement. As part of their standard procedures, Turnitin.com requires student papers to be archived in the company's database. Attorneys for the students point out that the papers are original works protected under federal copyright laws, and that Turnitin.com, by using these papers as part of their for-profit service, is violating the students' rights. Representatives for Turnitin point out that because only the student and instructor have access to a paper's contents, the student's rights are not violated. Some also object to Turnitin.com, believing that using such services can lead to an adversarial atmosphere in the classroom. Others, however, who have used services such as Turnitin.com, believe that such services can open the door for deeper conversations about plagiarism and academic integrity.

As educators grapple with how best to combat plagiarism in the Internet age, several high school students are suing a company that many districts and schools have hired to help them reduce such cheating. The lawsuit alleges that the company is violating the high school students' rights under U.S. copyright law. The students are required by their schools to submit some essays to Turnitin.com, a Web-based service that compares the documents against a massive internal database and other sources to look for signs of plagiarism. It then places the student works in an electronic archive.

Copyright Claims

The site's parent company, Oakland, Calif-based iParadigms LLC, submitted a motion April 26 [2007] to dismiss the case, which was filed in the U.S. District Court in Alexandria, Va. "Turnitin takes student papers and archives them, and they refuse not to archive them," said Robert A. Vanderhye, a lawyer from McLean, Va., who is representing the students pro bono [without charging a fee]. "Our clients have no problem . . . submitting documents for review. But when it comes to archiving, it raises a number of very serious issues, the first of which is copyright infringement."

John M. Barrie, the founder and chief executive officer of iParadigms, disagrees. "The use that we make of the students' papers comes under the 'fair use' clause of the U.S. Copyright Act," he said. The company also argues that the students, before submitting their papers, clicked "I agree" to contractual terms that release iParadigms from any liability.

Mr. Barrie said Turnitin receives about 100,000 student papers each day, and serves more than 7,000 educational institutions worldwide, including such top-ranked universities as Harvard and Georgetown. More than 4,500 U.S. high schools use Turnitin, he said. "Our users have validated us with their use," he said.

The lawsuit was filed by four unnamed students, two from McLean High School in Virginia and two from a high school in Arizona. It was originally filed March 27 [2007], and was

Some argue that antiplagiarism software violates the intellectual property rights of students because the programs require that papers be stored in the software companies' databases.

amended April 9. The legal action comes amid widespread concern among educators on how to address plagiarism as students can, with minimal effort, access a wealth of information and writing on the Internet and present it as their own work or without proper citation of sources.

"There is a great deal of temptation out there, and there are certain students who give in to that temptation because it's so easy," said Mary T. Christel, a veteran communication-arts teacher at Adlai E. Stevenson High School in Lincolnshire, Illinois, who uses the Turnitin service in her classes.

A study released last fall [2006] by the Josephson Institute of Ethics found that among more than 36,000 high school students surveyed, 60 percent said they had cheated on a test in the past year. One in three said they had used the Internet to plagiarize an assignment. The Los Angeles–based institute runs the character education program Character Counts.

Donald L. McCabe, a professor at Rutgers University's Newark, N.J., campus who studies plagiarism, said his own survey data of about 18,000 high schoolers over the past several years has shown troubling results, with about 60 percent of students admitting to some plagiarism. Most is of the "cut and paste" variety, he said, "a sentence here, a paragraph there, where they're taking from multiple sources and weaving in their own words."

Mr. McCabe said schools seem to take the problem of plagiarism seriously, but "a lot of them aren't sure what to do." The best approach, he argues, is to promote academic integrity to students. "I still think there's a place for Turnitin.com, but I'm opposed to its widespread use," he said. "To me that says to students, 'I can't trust any one of you.'"

How It Works

The starting point for the Turnitin "plagiarism prevention" program is an assignment's submission to the Web site by a student or teacher. Within 24 hours, the company sends the teacher an "originality report," based on what the company says is a search of billions of pages from current and archived items on the Internet, millions of student papers submitted to Turnitin, and commercial databases of journal articles and periodicals. The report shows the submitted paper along with matching sources. It includes percentage ratings for how similar it is to matching items and links to sources, but not to other archived student papers.

Each of the four students involved in the lawsuit obtained copyrights for academic papers they submitted to the Turnitin site, according to court papers, and the suit argues that the company's conduct infringes those protections. The plaintiffs seek $900,000 in damages from iParadigms.

Beyond objecting to the practice of archiving, the complaint says the company "may send a full and complete copy of a student's unpublished manuscript to an iParadigms client anywhere in the world upon request of the client, and without the student's permission."

But Mr. Barrie insists that student work is protected. "Only the student and their teacher will ever see this," he said of the student work. "The papers remain in the database." In its motion to dismiss the case, the defense focuses its argument on the fact that the students who are suing iParadigms agreed to release the company from liability.

"Instead of pursuing this school matter through the proper channels, plaintiffs have instead concocted a purported copyright claim," the motion says. A hearing on the motion was scheduled for May 11 [2007].

Fred von Lohmann, a staff lawyer at the Electronic Frontier Foundation, a San Francisco nonprofit organization that works to protect individuals' "digital rights," called the dispute interesting. "There are going to be many cases involving copying for the purposes of indexing," he predicted. A spokeswoman for the 164,000-student Fairfax County district in Virginia, which includes McLean High School, declined to comment on the suit, but said the district uses Turnitin both to help educate students about proper documentation of sources and to avoid plagiarism. The district first contracted with Turnitin in 2003; McLean High School began using the service last fall [2006].

Rebecca Moore Howard, an associate professor of writing and rhetoric at Syracuse University, said she worries Turnitin may deter good pedagogy and create an unhealthy classroom dynamic. "Turnitin is setting up faculty and students as enemies," she said. "Students are having to prove that they're innocent, and that's a terrible classroom environment to be establishing."

But Turnitin appears popular with educators in many schools, based on the large subscriber base. Mr. Barrie says that the renewal rate is above 95 percent, and that the client base is growing quickly.

A Platform

Keith D. Klein, an English teacher at Washington Lee High School in Arlington, Va., says he tries to find teachable moments in his occasional use of the service with students. "I let them know what the Web site does, what it is," he said. "That in itself is a platform for me to talk about plagiarism, and a pretty good disincentive [for the practice]."

Mr. Klein has been using Turnitin for several years, but his use has evolved. Turnitin offers several services beyond the antiplaglarism feature, including one that allows a peer review of student work by their classmates. "I don't use it anymore as a 'gotcha' mechanism, but more as a deterrent," Mr. Klein said. "I also like to use it because it's got a pretty good peer-review aspect to it. I use it in that way."

Ms. Christel, the Illinois teacher, said she doesn't use Turnitin for all assignments, but routinely uses it when students submit major papers. "Prior to Turnitin.com, it took a fairly large chunk of my time with some student papers when I suspected there was some kind of citation issue," she said. "It allows me to focus on other issues than playing detective."

Ms. Christel stressed that Turnitin isn't the only tool she uses to reduce plagiarism, and that overall, teachers need to work hard to ensure students understand what plagiarism is and how to avoid it. "It's got to get started very early on," she said, "It needs to be something we do on a consistent basis, and that we're constantly reinforcing."

What You Should Know About Plagiarism

What Plagiarism Is

- Buying, borrowing, or stealing a research paper or essay and presenting it as your own.
- Putting someone else's ideas, argument, or outline into your own words and presenting it as your own.
- Using word-for-word someone else's phrases, sentences, or paragraphs without giving credit.
- Putting into your own words someone else's phrases, sentences, or paragraphs without giving credit.
- Presenting facts or statistics without citing the source.

Facts About Plagiariasm

- Both off-the-shelf and custom-written college admission essays, research papers, master's theses, and doctoral dissertations are available for purchase over the Internet.
- About 1 percent of the papers processed every day by Turnitin are completely copied, and about 29 percent contain significant plagiarism.
- The 2006 Josephson Institute Report Card on the Ethics of American Youth indicates that:
  - Thirty-three percent of high school students copied from the Internet at least once during the previous year, and 18 percent copied more than once.
  - Sixty percent cheated on a test at least once during the previous year, and 35 percent cheated more than once.

- The most recent surveys conducted by Rutgers University professor Donald McCabe indicate that:
  - Almost 58 percent of eighteen thousand high school students admitted to cut-and-paste Internet plagiarism.
  - Twenty-one percent of college students have cheated on a test or exam in a significant way.
  - Fifty-one percent have cheated on written work in a significant way.
  - Four out of five students who had cheated on written assignments have done it with the help of the Internet.
  - Forty-four percent of students believe that cutting and pasting from the Internet is not really cheating.
  - Forty-four percent of college professors have ignored clear cases of cheating in their own classes.
- An article published in *Education Week* reports that 54 percent of college students surveyed admitted to Internet plagiarism and that 47 percent believe that their professors ignore cheating.
- In a 2001 survey of 246 graduate students, 55 percent admitted to plagiarism by paraphrasing, 16 percent to word-for-word plagiarism, and less than 5 percent to submitting a paper they had purchased from the Internet or copied from another student.

What You Should Do About Plagiarism

Most students, educators, and professional writers would agree on a basic definition of plagiarism, that it is wrong, and that it is prevalent. But what should be done about it? Do students need better teachers, or do teachers need better students? Is a commercial product like Turnitin the answer, or does giving Turnitin access to student papers violate students' rights?

Plagiarism can be a complicated issue, but it is worth understanding. As a student, how can you make sure that you really understand it? As a member of an educational community, how can you know if your school is taking the right approach? What you do about it may be the difference between your academic success and failure.

Understand Plagiarism

Whether an increase in plagiarism is the result of poor teaching or poor students is not the most important issue if you are the one facing the penalties. The most important thing is that you understand what plagiarism is. Ask your teacher for a definition. If the concept still is not clear, ask your school counselor where to go for more help, read a book or several books about it, study one or two of the thousands of Internet resources provided by college academic help centers, or even do an interactive Internet tutorial.

Before you hand in an assignment, ask another teacher or a family member to look it over and check it for originality. Provide them with the sources that you consulted, so they can make sure that you have used your own words. If your teacher marks you down or fails you for plagiarism, insist on an explanation and ask questions until you are sure that you understand. Then rewrite the assignment and ask your teacher to reevaluate it, whether you will get credit for it or not.

Research Policies

How does your school view plagiarism? Your school should have a student handbook or conduct code that explains its definition of and penalties for plagiarism as well as procedures for appeal. Is your teacher *required* to allow you to rewrite your assignment for credit? You will not know unless you find out your school's policies regarding plagiarism. Some policies are more detailed and comprehensive than others. If a policy is vague or unclear, ask for clarification.

Understand the Debate

How do other schools similar to yours approach plagiarism? If their policies are not available online, most schools are willing to provide you with a copy of their student handbook. You can also read the articles compiled in this book and listed in the bibliography to see what other schools are doing to try to solve the plagiarism problem and if their methods are helping or seem better than the approach that your school is taking.

Examine Your Own Views

What motivates you? Under what circumstances might you plagiarize when you normally would not? Would an honor code motivate you to be more honest? Would the threat of expulsion make you think twice about presenting someone else's work as your own? Do you think that a school has the right to use a for-profit company like Turnitin to look for plagiarism? Do the policies at your school seem to be working? Are other students cutting and pasting from the Internet or sharing papers without being caught or without understanding that it is plagiarism? Are teachers looking the other way? Is that okay with you?

Take a Stand

As you read the articles in this volume and consider the issues that they raise, you are developing an informed view of the topic. The first place that you can take a stand on the topic of plagiarism is in your own work. As you come to understand what plagiarism is, refuse to settle for it in your writing. You have the skills necessary to give credit to your sources or to discover how to do so.

Get to know your school's policies on plagiarism. If policies do not exist, or if they are not very clear, speak up. Teachers, school counselors, and administrators are concerned about this issue, too. Most will welcome your interest. Should you find, though, that your school has existing policies that do not seem fair or reasonable in light of your study on the subject, do not be afraid to speak up. You may have insights that others have not considered. Just remember to do so in a reasoned and respectful manner, so that your thoughts are not dismissed without a thorough hearing.

American Historical Association
400 A St. SE, Washington, DC 20003-3889
(202) 544-2422
e-mail: info@historians.org
Web site: www.historians.org

The American Historical Association is the largest historical association in the United States. Founded in 1884, it continues to maintain historical documents, conduct historical research, offer resources to historians and educators, and monitor standards in the profession. It adopted an updated Statement on Standards of Conduct in 2005, which includes a section on plagiarism.

American Psychological Association (APA)
750 First St. NE, Washington, DC 20002-4242
(800) 374-2721 or (202) 336-5500
Web site: http://apastyle.apa.org

The APA has developed a citation style that is used consistently in psychology publications as well as in other social science disciplines. The APA has also developed an ethics code that covers plagiarism as well as other ethical issues important to the field of psychology.

The Center for Academic Integrity (CAI)
126 Hardin Hall, Clemson University, Clemson, SC 29634-5138
(864) 656-1293
e-mail: CAI-L@clemson.edu
Web site: www.academicintegrity.org

With an emphasis on higher and secondary education, the CAF is focused on the evolving issues of academic integrity. Its main purpose is to encourage students, faculty, and administrators to be actively committed to academic integrity and to provide research and resources to that end. Its Web site provides links to down-loadable pamphlets, educational materials, and articles along with links to other online resources.

Character Counts!
National Office / Josephson Institute of Ethics
9841 Airport Blvd., #300, Los Angeles, CA 90045
(310) 846-4800
Web site: www.charactercounts.org

Administrated by the Josephson Institute of Ethics, Character Counts! is a character education program used by thousands of schools and community organizations. Based on six pillars: trust-worthiness, respect, responsibility, fairness, caring, and citizen-ship, the organization provides materials and support to member organizations. Free resources are also available through their Web site, including an "Avoiding Plagiarism" video and quiz.

Josephson Institute of Ethics
9841 Airport Blvd., #300, Los Angeles, CA 90045
(310) 846-4800
Web site: www.josephsoninstitute.org

The Josephson Institute addresses issues of both individual and organizational integrity. It seeks to equip and empower honesty in classrooms, in sports, in law enforcement, and in corporate pol-icy making. In addition to educational materials and seminars in ethics, the Josephson Institute's Web site also maintains a collec-tion of reports and speeches on ethical issues.

The Online Writing Lab at Purdue (OWL)
e-mail: http://owl.english.purdue.edu
Web site: http://owl.english.purdue.edu

OWL is perhaps the most well-known university online writing help Web site and is available to the public. At no cost, the Writing Lab at Purdue University provides written resources for both students and instructors as well as access to OWL Mail Tutors for brief writing questions. Included in their site is a section on avoiding plagiarism with both information and an exercise.

Oregon School Library Information Service (OSLIS)
Web site: www.oslis.org

OSLIS is a cooperative venture between the Oregon Association of School Libraries and the University of Washington's iSchool. OSLIS serves as a research and writing resource for public school students and their teachers. Among the resources available are writing style sheets and online programs that help students with proper citation.

Ryerson University Academic Integrity Website
350 Victoria St., Toronto, ON, Canada M5B 2K3
(416) 979-5000
e-mail: aio@ryerson.ca
Web site: www.ryerson.ca

Ryerson University's academic integrity Web site offers information, tutorials, and quizzes. The tutorials are presented in five episodes featuring students trying to maneuver their way through academic ethical situations, including unintentional plagiarism.

University of Michigan Searchpath
Web site: www.lib.umich.edu

The University of Michigan has made public this online interactive tutorial with self-quizzes and online handouts. It covers citing sources and plagiarism as well as other research and writing topics.

Vaughan Memorial Library, Acadia University: "You Quote It, You Note It!"
Web site: http://library.acadian.ca

This humorous online interactive tutorial explains what plagiarism is, gives students practice identifying plagiarism, and explains how to properly cite sources.

BIBLIOGRAPHY

Books

David Callahan, *The Cheating Culture: Why More Americans Are Doing Wrong to Get Ahead.* Orlando, FL: Harcourt, 2004.

Dougie Child, *Product Versus Product: The Term Paper Industry and the New Face of Cheating in American Education.* Bangor, ME: Booklocker.com, 2005.

Barbara Francis, *Other People's Words: What Plagiarism Is and How to Avoid It.* Berkeley Heights, NJ: Enslow, 2005.

Ann Graham Gaines, *Don't Steal Copyrighted Stuff! Avoiding Plagiarism and Illegal Internet Downloading.* Berkeley Heights, NJ: Enslow, 2007.

Robert A. Harris, *Using Sources Effectively: Strengthening Your Writing and Avoiding Plagiarism.* Los Angeles: Pyrczak, 2005.

Thomas Jewell, *Prentice Hall's Guide to Understanding Plagiarism.* Upper Saddle River, NJ: Pearson, 2004.

Julia Johns and Sarah Keller, *Cite It Right: The SourceAid Guide to Citation, Research, and Avoiding Plagiarism.* Osterville, MA: SourceAid, 2007.

Ann Lathrop and Kathleen Foss, *Guiding Students from Cheating and Plagiarism to Honesty and Integrity: Strategies for Change.* Westport, CT: Libraries Unlimited, 2005.

James D. Lester, *Research Paper Handbook: Your Complete Guide.* Tuscon, AZ: Good Year Books, 2005.

Charles Lipson, *Doing Honest Work in College: How to Prepare Citations, Avoid Plagiarism, and Achieve Real Academic Success.* Chicago: University of Chicago Press, 2004.

Richard A. Posner, *The Little Book of Plagiarism.* New York: Pantheon, 2007.

Herbert Ulysses Quickwit, *Plagiarizm: How Profs Spot a Cheat.* Lincoln, NE: iUniverse, 2004.

Linda Stern, *What Every Student Should Know About Avoiding Plagiarism*. New York: Longman, 2006.

Periodicals

Jamaal Abdul-Alim, "Internet Cheating Clicks with Students: More Plagiarizers Using Technology for Unfair Edge," *Milwaukee Journal Sentinel*, December 13, 2006.

Kurt Anderson, "Generation Xerox: Youth May Not be an Excuse for Plagiarism. But it is an Explanation," *New York Magazine*, May 15. 2006.

William Badke, "Give Plagiarism the Weight it Deserves." *Online* 31, no. 5, September/October 2007: 58–60.

Jon Baggaley and Bob Spencer, "The Mind of a Plagiarist," *Learning, Media and Technology*, March 2005.

Thomas Bartlett and Scott Smallwood, "Mentor vs. Protégé: The Professor Published the Student's Work as His Own. What's Wrong with That?" *Chronicle of Higher Education*, December 17, 2004.

Shifra Baruchson-Arbib and Eti Yaari, "Printed Versus Internet Plagiarism: A Study of Students' Perception," *International Journal of Information Ethics*, June 2004.

Burton Bollag, "Edward Waters College Loses Accreditation Following Plagiarism Scandal," *Chronicle of Higher Education*, December 9, 2004.

Michael Bugeja, "Don't Let Students Overlook Internet Plagiarism," *Education Digest*, October 2004.

Shawn G. Clouthier, "Institutionalized Plagiarism," *Scientist*, August 2, 2004.

K. Matthew Dames, "Plagiarism: The New 'Piracy,'" *Information Today*, November 2006.

Karoun Demirjian, "What Is the Price of Plagiarism?" *Christian Science Monitor*, May 11, 2006.

Bruce Flamm, "Third Strike for Columbia University Prayer Study: Plagiarism," *Skeptical Inquirer*, May/June 2007.

Roxie L. Foster, "Avoiding Unintentional Plagiarism," *Journal for Specialists in Pediatric Nursing*, January 2007.

Felicia R. Lee, "Are More People Cheating? Despite Ample Accounts of Dishonesty, a Moral Decline Is Hard to Calculate," *New York Times*, October 4, 2003.

Jonathan Letham, "The Ecstasy of Influence: A Plagiarism," *Harpers*, February 2007.

Thomas G. Long, "Stolen Goods: Tempted to Plagiariaze: Preaching Depends on Trust. When We Deceive Listeners, We Undermine the Basis of Our Witness," *Christian Century*, April 17, 2007.

Colleen MacDonnell, "The Problem of Plagiarism: Students May not Know They've Committed an Offense," *School Library Journal*, January 2005.

Douglas MacMillan, "Looking Over Turnitin's Shoulder; a Tech Tool for Detecting Plagiarism Has Received Some Low Marks from Users Concerned About Privacy and the Service's Accuracy," *Business Week Online*, March 13, 2007.

Donald McCabe, "It Takes a Village: Academic Honesty," *Liberal Education*, Summer/Fall 2005.

Paul Mooney, "Plagued by Plagiarism," *Chronicle of Higher Education*, May 19, 2006.

Jon Pareles, "Plagiarism in Dylan, or a Cultural Collage?" *New York Times*, July 12, 2003.

Julie Rawe, "A Question of Honor," *Time*, May 28, 2007.

Kelley R. Taylor, "Cheater, Cheater . . . ," *Principal Leadership*, April 2003.

Matt Villano, "Taking the Work Out of Homework," *T.H.E. Journal*, October 2006.

May Wong, "New Software Detects Plagiarized Passages," *USA Today*, April 6, 2004.

INDEX

T

Teachers. *See* Faculty

Term papers

costs of buying, 38

custom written, 35, 37–39

plagiarism detection services
for, 60

purchased online, 30–31,
34–40, 58, 62

purchasing of, 13–14, 33–34

testing for plagiarism, 30–31,
39, 60, 70–71

Thompson, Michael, 74

Totenberg, Nina, 14

Tribe, Laurence, 54

Trust, 66

Turnitin.com

custom papers and, 38

lawsuits against, 81–84

popularity of, 84–85

service offered by, 71, 83–84

use of, 30–31, 60, 85

U

Universities. *See* Colleges and
universities

University of California, 71–72

University of Iowa, 30

University of Maryland, 30

University of Michigan, 73

University of Notre Dame, 60

University of Virginia, 29–30,
70

V

Vanderhye, Robert A., 81

Viswanathan, Kaavya, 5, 7, 17,
18

W

Wagner, Glenn, 7

Warger, Tom, 68

Washington and Lee
University, 29–30, 31

Watkins, Dawn, 31

Wcopyfind, 70

Web sites

critique of, 35–36

See also Internet plagiarism;
Online services

White lies, 42

Williams, Renee, 27

Writer's manuals, 13

A Writer's Reference (Hacker),
72

Writing, elements of good, 5

Wurtzel, Elizabeth, 15

Z

Zakarian, John, 72